Bogies and Billygoats

Bogies and Billygoats

◆

A History of the Albany Municipal Golf Course

By Eric Bryant

Writers Club Press
New York Lincoln Shanghai

Bogies and Billygoats
A History of the Albany Municipal Golf Course

Writers Club Press
an imprint of iUniverse, Inc.

For information address:
iUniverse, Inc.
2021 Pine Lake Road, Suite 100
Lincoln, NE 68512
www.iuniverse.com

ISBN: 0-595-26450-6

Printed in the United States of America

This book is dedicated to my mother.

"It's certainly the sportiest I've ever played and it is no place for the weak knees, sister! A Rocky Mountain goat would be winded if he chased around that near nine."

—Unidentified Albany Muny golfer, 1932

Contents

Thanks

Thanks to all who took the time to speak with me about the golf course:

Deborah Campbell, John Boyd Thacher III, Betty Thacher, Jack McEneny, Frank Cummings, Bob Huba, Ed Huba, Al Huba, Frank Hoeffner, Tom Delaney, Peter Van Kampen, Larry White, Lou Weinman, Joe Rafferty, Bob Kisselback, Charlie Murphy, Mike Daniels, Ginny Ruszas, Charlie Ruszas, Jack Vogel, Larry White, George Cinney, Geraldine Zwack, Tom Patterson, Tom Vidulich, Steve Vatter, Scott Gallup, Peter Gerard, Jim Jeffers, the staff of the Albany Public Library and the Albany Institute of History and Art, Patty Bryce and Craig Carlson of the Albany County Hall of Records, Richard Barrett, Bob Smith, Ed Bosse, and Dan Hershberg.

Special thanks to Mike Larabee, an old friend and a top shelf editor. I wish I had the time to write that first chapter, Mike.

A final big thank you to my wife Kathleen and sons, Owen and Ben. Thanks for sleeping so soundly during your naps so that I could write.

Introduction

Somewhere along the line, this place got under my skin.

Maybe it was that rain-soaked afternoon in the early 1980s when I reached the old sixth hole and decided to trudge on. I nearly holed the tee shot, ran down the gully in a downpour and missed the three-foot birdie. I yelled at the heavens, cursing my yips in the rain.

Ten years later, I approached the "new" 18th following a solo, bogey-laden round. I overshot the green and had nothing but trouble to get down. My mind and wedge went into a kind of symbiotic overdrive and for a brief moment before hitting the ball, I was absolutely sure that it would fall in the cup. It did. There I was, alone on a golf course, with the sun fading. I looked up to the golf ghosts who haunt this place and said, "Thank you."

The place was already getting to me.

In winter, with the course closed, I would walk the abandoned holes of the old muny, trying to recount their path, finding in the thicket the remains of Top Flites and Club Specials half-hidden in mud; finding Pabst Blue Ribbon cans rusting in the woods; discovering that this place had a history written in those objects. Who sliced that Spalding Dot into the woods bordering No. 3? Who climbed the muny gullies, beer can in hand? As I walked, I imagined their rounds, their drinking, their lousy golf games and the random, heroic shots that kept them coming back.

I walked the old course with a fully fueled imagination, and I walked it often. My shag bag overflowed with ancient balata. I began thinking of the course as my private hideaway, a place where I felt most peaceful, lost in the imagined wanderings of some long-gone duffers.

Unlike nearly all of the people I talked to for this book, I was not a "muny kid," a 36-hole-a-day-playing golf junkie. My obsession with the game, and later, my fixation with the place once known as the Albany Municipal Golf Course, began slowly in high school, and then accelerated when I returned to live in Albany in my twenties.

Among the few times I played the course when I was a teenager, my partner was John Thacher, a neighborhood kid from down the street and, more importantly, the great-grandnephew of the man who had the foresight to create the place back in the 1930s, Albany Mayor John Boyd Thacher II.

John never met his namesake, but he knew his history and family lore. As we played, he would talk about this and that. He mentioned the old eighth hole—uphill par three, two-tiered green—that it was once considered one of the toughest par threes in the country. Even then, I was hooked.

Years later, on random winter weekends, I began the first tentative searches that led to this book. Poring over microfilmed newspapers at the Albany Public Library, I wanted to know more about this collection of hills and gullies known as Albany Muny. I thought I would be satisfied filling in a few facts behind the movie screen imagination of my mind. But I was wrong. The answers I found in musty newspaper clippings simply led to other questions. Why would they pick such a godforsaken property for a golf course? What was this land used for before it was a golf course? Who were the characters that played here? Who was this Jerry Dwyer everyone talked about?

I got the names of a few old timers and called them, but they were wary. "You want to write a book about what?" they asked. I didn't push the issue.

I put up one of those pull-off tab notices in the hall next to the men's locker room, asking people to call me if they had any stories about the "old course." When I returned two months later, all of the little tabs with my phone number had been taken, but no one called. I put up another poster, same result. Trips to the library microfilm room became less frequent, and discouragement set in. My little golf course history project was falling by the wayside.

Still, the Muny was my refuge.

More trips to the golf course—summer days with random rounds, practice sessions on the old 18th green, winter walks through the vales of the inward nine. The place still had me in its grip, and by now I was convinced those golf ghosts were pleading with me not to drop the story. I made a few more phone calls, which began to snowball, and I started banging out what little information I already accumulated. Up to now, I had considered the project a hobby. When I began having cloud-filled dreams about teeing off on the old first tee, I knew it had become an obsession.

Knowing golfers as a fairly obsessive bunch, I wasn't surprised to eventually find others who shared my passion for the old Muny. The place was, and still is, a haven for Albany golfers; a place to lay down a few bucks and forget your troubles. What surprised me was the truly rich history of the old course.

More than a few top-notch golfers were introduced to the game here and their stories carry both comedy and tragedy. Joe Ruszas, a Muny caddy from the 1930s, went on to win the New York State Amateur in 1944. Two of the area's top teaching professionals—Peter Gerard of Orchard Creek and Jim Jeffers of Eagle Crest—started out as "muny kids," and they're damn proud of it. The same could be said for the crop of Albany youngsters who dominated junior golf in the early 1960s. Charlie Murphy and Mike Daniels, two from that crowd, will tell you that the Muny was their golfing refuge as teenagers. Jerry Dwyer, the jovial, chain-smoking professional who manned the clubhouse for more than 30 years, deserves a book all to himself. He became a legend for his ability to teach almost anyone how to play the game.

For many who frequented the Muny, it was more than just a golf course. It was a home away from home. The clubhouse bar became an unofficial headquarters for at least two generations of city politicos, and Albany's patronage system flourished at the course under the regime of Corning and O'Connell.

People loved and loathed the Albany Municipal Golf Course in equal measure. Without question, the place was a pretty rundown track, but for those who appreciated the game, it didn't matter. It was their golf course, and for 60 years they came to play.

◆   ◆   ◆

Since I could find little official documentation from the city about the history of the Albany Municipal Golf Course, nearly all of the information contained in this book was obtained through secondary sources and personal interviews. I did try to double check facts, but the truthfulness of some anecdotes and stories I will leave to the reader's judgment. I'd like to believe Al Capone once paid $1,000 to have the front nine to himself for a day, but even if that story isn't true, it's still part of the Muny lore.

Most of the early part of the book doesn't have much to do with golf. Since I became fascinated with the land itself, I wanted to set a foundation for what was to come later. If you're simply a golf junkie, you can skip the first few chapters, although there are some interesting facts that may be of interest to history buffs and Albany residents.

I've included a few chapters on the evolution of golf in the Capital District and the short-lived and little known miniature golf craze that swept through the country in 1930.

The middle portion of the book is a series of oral histories taken from golfers and others who have roamed the fairways over the past 70 years. These are broken down by decades, roughly based on when the interviewees spent their time at the course. Toward the back of the book, the three layouts are examined hole-by-hole, and there is a list of city champions—winners of the Mayor's Cup from 1932 to 2002. I've included only women's city champs from recent years because it seemed the women's title was contested rather sporadically in the bygone era. Anyone who would like to help me collect a more comprehensive list of female city champs is welcome to join the task.

I also was able to pull together some facts on the club professionals and caddies who have worked the course over the decades, most notably Jerry Dwyer, whose tenure lasted some 30 years. My apologies to the current pro, Steve Vatter. Steve, I guess you haven't been here long enough to be "historic," but I'm sure you'll add some lore of your own to the course in the years to come.

While I was wrapping up the writing, I walked into the pro shop and noticed an architecturally drawn course map that outlined several updates and changes on the layout. These alterations started in late summer 2002 and they will be ongoing through the next year. I'm excited to see the course still evolving, but I didn't mention any of those changes in the hole-by-hole descriptions. I guess it shows you can't keep up with the history of a place that's constantly changing.

◆　　◆　　◆

I am confident there are numerous events, people and stories and that were left out of this book. I tried to talk to as many folks as I could, but I have a full-time job and two kids to raise. Finishing this book may have been an obsession, but it was researched and written whenever I could find the time. If you do have an "old Muny" story to tell, I'd still like to hear it.

Eric Bryant, December 2002

Before the Course

In 1854, the poet Henry Wadsworth Longfellow penned these words, one of the opening stanzas from his epic poem "The Song of Hiawatha."

> "In the vale of Tawasentha,
> In the green and silent valley,
> By the pleasant water-courses,
> Dwelt the singer Nawadaha.
> Round about the Indian village
> Spread the meadows and the corn-fields,
> And beyond them stood the forest,
> Stood the groves of singing pine-trees,
> Green in Summer, white in Winter,
> Ever sighing, ever singing."

The Vale of Tawasentha. The banks of the Normanskill. One and the same? Perhaps and perhaps not. Normanside Country Club, which is situated directly across from the Albany Municipal Golf Course, founded its reputation on the fact that Wadsworth, one of America's greatest 19th century poets, was speaking of the upper Normanskill, its "green and silent valley" and "pleasant water courses." The club's logo even shows a stately native, with the crest "Tawasentha" below. One of the area's nicest par-3 courses also slopes along the Normanskill out in Guilderland. Its name: Hiawatha Trails.

Does this matter to you? Probably not. Whether Longfellow's Hiawatha was from Albany or northern Minnesota (the other possible

Tawasentha), the poem speaks of a mystical place, haunted by nature's spirits. Indisputable is the fact that Native Americans hunted, fished and built communities along the banks of the Normanskill Creek well before western civilization found its way across the Atlantic.

Walk into the golf course's clubhouse and you'll find proof. The arrowhead collection of Richard Burturba has been on display in a locked glass case since the new building was erected in 1990. Burturba's finds—projectile points, notched tools, and other Pre-Colombian artifacts—were picked up on or near the golf course during his lifetime of amateur archaeology. It's clear evidence that your wayward tee shot on the 14th hole may have landed in what was once an Indian encampment. According to Burturba's finds, Native Americans roamed through, or settled along, the northern banks of the Normans Kill as far back as 3000 B.C., and they were here pretty much through the next 4,800 years.

An archaeological report offered up prior to the new course being constructed showed significant prehistoric settlements along the banks of the creek. Remnants of "prehistoric hunting camps" were found seven to 10 inches below ground in the areas of the current 14th and 15th greens. The report, compiled by the archaeological firm Collamer and Associates, found several notched points and some debris that would indicate the area was a way station for generations of hunters. Although the site had been disturbed by several centuries of farming, Collamer concluded that it "appears to have a significant degree of integrity." The report recommended that the site either be fully excavated or buried to preserve it intact. Luckily, for golfers at least, the city decided on the latter.

The area along the banks of the creek was so well used, in fact, that a classification of arrowhead called the Normanskill type is well known among North American archaeologists. The rough twin notched projectile is usually dated to the Late Archaic Period, somewhere between 3000 and 1400 B.C. That's a long time before you or I took our first swing at the old course.

Open your mind's eye a bit and the history of the land is easy to picture, actually—a small community of Native Americans encamped for the summer along the Normans Kill, setting traps and fishing the creek. Their children playing along the valleys and ridges that crisscross the golf course. Maybe one young boy or girl over those 5,000 years picked up a stick and tried to hit a rock farther than a friend.

In the years before Western arrival, the land in the Capital District, in fact up and down the entire Eastern Seaboard, was dominated by forests—those "groves of singing pine trees" of which Longfellow wrote. And the area surrounding the Capital District was a well-known Indian meeting place, being the confluence of two major navigable waterways—the Mohawk and Hudson rivers. From around the year 1000 A.D. through the next three centuries, the Mahican tribe dominated the region. Around 1300, the great Iroquoian nation slowly began overtaking the Mahicans, although the tribe remained an active population in the area for the next 500 years. Mohawk, Oneidas and other tribes shared this land until the arrival of western settlers in the 17th century.

When Henry Hudson first sailed up his namesake river in September 1609, his Halve Moone weighed anchor just below the entrance to what was soon to be called the Normans Kill Creek. Hudson was looking for the mythical passage to India and China but found, more practically, a nice place to trade for beaver pelts and other native riches. At the time, Indians were still living along the banks of the Normans Kill, as related in the family history of Albert Andrissen Bradt de Noorman, who settled on the creek in the middle of the 17th century. As you might expect, de Noorman was Norwegian, from the city of Fredrikstad. His mill was located on the lower Normanskill, closer to where the creek empties into the Hudson. In a volume titled *"Descendants of Albert and Arent Andriessen Bradt,"* published in 1990, it's noted that there was a sawmill in 1637 operated by the family on what was called the Tawasentha, (there's that name again) and by 1646 Arent had dropped out of the picture and Albert had become the owner of two sawmills on the creek. His standing in the community became so strong that the creek was soon known as Noorman's Kill; our own Normanskill.

All of this likely has little interest to the casual golfer strolling along the fairways, but it's stated for a reason. The land we hack and curse across, where we settle to enjoy the rolling course of the creek or yell in celebration of a birdie putt, has a history before us.

◆   ◆   ◆

In some circles, if you even hint that golf originated somewhere outside Scotland, you'll be for a long night of argument or at least a few good pokes in the face. There is absolutely no doubt that the Scots nurtured and made the game of golf famous, and anyone who's walked the hallowed fairways of St. Andrew's would attest that the game has a rightful birthplace on the Firth of Fife.

But the Dutch, long known for odd sporting customs, (one traditional game involved grabbing a greased-up goose while riding by it on a horse) have a hand in this game as well. And, as our lands are Dutch in origin, it's worth a brief explaining of how Albany was once a hotbed of what the Dutch called "kolf" or "kolven."

"Kolf", the sport, resembled today's golf somewhat like ice fishing resembles fly fishing. There is a rod and reel and the goal is to catch fish, but there the similarity ends. With club, ball and target at a distance, kolf was played on city streets and also on the ice of the frozen Hudson River. In a June 1996 *Times Union* article, staff writer Paul Grondahl noted that the fledgling game was banned for a time in old Beverwyck, perhaps, in part, because of one incident that could be called "kolf-induced assault."

Grondahl quoted Charles Gehring, director of the New Netherland Project at the State Library, who published a scholarly article involving the wedding day troubles of Philip Pietersz Schuyler, a prominent 17th century fur trader in the city. In what may have been a Dutch version of the bachelor party, Schuyler was out on the ice with his buddies, December 12, 1650, playing a little kolf. When his group returned to a city tavern to settle up the day's Nassau, an argument broke out among the contestants.

"A knife was brandished. Schuyler, the bridegroom, was punched in the head. Gijsbert Cornelisz was stabbed," Grondahl wrote.

Since the common wager was usually on brandy, the argument can probably be blamed on heavy drinking rather than bad kolfing. Nine years after the incident, city leaders decided to ban kolf on city streets, and the game took on an outlaw status.

Sixty-five years before Grondahl's piece, and during a nationwide craze for miniature golf, another *Times Union* article claimed, as its headline read, "Golf Game Originated in Albany, Not Scotland."

"Here's what a National Geographic society bulletin had to say recently: 'Miniature golf is not new to these shores. Early chroniclers tell of the Dutch burghers playing 'kolf' on small courses near taverns," the March 17, 1931 article reads. "After a round or two, the 'kolfers' retired to the tavern for a bowl of punch, lingering over it in typical nineteenth hole fashion until the room was filled with the aroma of their long clay pipes."

Real golf in the Capital District began some two centuries after the Dutch gave up power for good. But that's for a later chapter. There is plenty of evidence to show that hitting a ball with a stick was, for a time, a common Albany pastime several centuries before the turn of the 20th century.

Hurstville

Before there was an Albany Municipal Golf Course, before the city of Albany even reached out to take in the farms and byways of western New Scotland Avenue, there was Hurstville.

It was a small town on the edge of a growing city, a place of road-houses and trolley cars, plain-shingled schools and dairy farms, one of which became the eventual site of Albany Muny.

Like most places whose names are not bound by municipal lines, Hurstville was a gathering of homes and farms rather than a village proper. In general, it was the area bisected by New Scotland, Krumkill and Whitehall roads. Split through by a wood plank toll road which left Madison Avenue and extended through Bethlehem and out into Schoharie, it was farmed and settled mostly by German immigrants in the early and mid-19th century. According to local historian Allison Bennett, one of the road's old toll booths was once located directly across from the entrance to the golf course.

Hurstville at the turn of the last century sounds like a sleepy outpost, but it had its hotspots. *The Albany Hand-Book of 1881* mentions the "famous Log Tavern" at the corner of Whitehall and New Scotland. What it was famous for wasn't mentioned, but taverns aren't usually notorious for high culture. Namesake William Hurst opened Hurst's Hotel on the site of the Log Tavern, and beginning in 1861, he also ran a racetrack for trotters in the hamlet.

Bennett, in her book *Bethlehem Revisited,* notes that the hotel was a popular Prohibition hangout, but by then it had acquired a much more colorful name—"The Love Nest."

"It is easy to picture couples in roadsters with rumble seats, dancing the Charleston and the Black Bottom," Bennett writes, but the dance didn't last long. The Love Nest burned down on Election Day 1929, just before Albany Muny was to show its face.

Many of the area's original landowners—Hurst, Kakely, Etling, to name a few—are remembered in the residential street names of the area, now the southwestern end of the city of Albany. O'Neil Road, which leads into the golf course, was named for the farm owned by Peter O'Neil, a dairyman whose house once stood near today's seventh green. Take a look down the embankment some 100 feet to the left of that green and you'll find more than old golf balls. It's a decaying trash pile of farm family junk—old barrels, medicine bottles, pieces of twisted metal and tools. It was this farm that young Ed Huba and his brothers used to sneak to for a low-cost glass of buttermilk when they were playing the old course back in the 1930s. The dirt road that runs down the left side of today's driving range once led to the O'Neil farm. The O'Neils may not have been the first to farm the land along the northern bank of the Normanskill on today's golf course. The *New Topographical Maps of the Counties of Albany and Schenectady*, printed in 1866, shows a lonely little homestead near the same location, owned by an A. Booth. A small farm? Maybe a mill? There's no formal road leading to the home, just a dotted dash noting a path to civilization along the muddy creek.

Although they would be today, O'Neil and his neighbors were not City of Albany residents. Hurstville, and its entire neighboring burg, Karlsfeld, further up New Scotland, were part of the Town of Bethlehem until the latter part of the 20th century. Albany's municipal golf course was actually built in Bethlehem on land purchased by the city.

Following a trend in other parts of North Bethlehem, Karlsfeld was officially ceded from town to city in 1967. Residents along New Scotland had been petitioning Mayor Erastus Corning to take over the land so that they could receive municipal water and sewer services. Corning eventually granted their wish and the city's border bulged to the Normanskill, where it's remained ever since.

Few today would know the name of the little hamlet of Karlsfeld except for a now-faded sign on New Scotland Road telling travelers to slow their motorized pace. As a kid, I thought the sign reading "KARLSFELD SLOW" meant the people there weren't too bright.

The hamlet's most dominating structure is the New York State Corrections Training Academy, and its adjoining swath of green grass. The impressive building was constructed as the Mater Christi Seminary and opened in 1954. The land previously was owned by the parish of St. Vincent De Paul Church, one of the city's largest Catholic congregations, and used as a recreation center. In 1930, the parish purchased the land, and a year later held formal dedication ceremonies for the recreation fields.

◆   ◆   ◆

Probably the most impressive and most visible sign of the past along upper New Scotland Avenue is the Walley Farm, the once white, now clean brick home just to the right of O'Neil Road. Current owner Deborah Campbell said she's seen documents dating the structure to the early 19th century, but she believes portions of the house may be even older. The Campbells have lived in the house, once owned by author and Nelson Rockefeller biographer Joseph Persico, since the early 1970s.

Older muni golfers fondly remember the Walley Farm, which sold annual and perennial flowers as well as produce until the 1950s. Al Walley was the last living member of his family who kept a farm on New Scotland Road, but his lineage stretches back at least a few generations. The 1866 county map shows Walleys up and down what is today's New Scotland Road, and out near the junction of two local waterways, the Normanskill and the Crum Kill. Campbell thinks an older white clapboard house still standing further up New Scotland Road (970 New Scotland) may also have been a Walley residence. It's likely that the farm stretched down to today's Hartman Road, and it once included an impressive barn, which stood near the corner of O'Neil Road and Par Circle. The barn was torn down in the 1960s to make room for the growing subdivision that sprung up at the course's entrance.

By the 1960s, when the Corning land purchase took place, Albany had well and truly stretched its reach out New Scotland Avenue. Gone were the trolleys and truck farms of Hurstville, now replaced by single-family homes and small shops. The 1950s brought the New York State Thruway through the tiny hamlet, effectively cutting the O'Neil Farm off from its neighbors on Whitehall Road. The hilly slopes in front of the dairy farm had a purpose however.

By 1957, the Albany Municipal Golf Course had been in operation for 25 years, and was enjoying a reputation, not for its excellent conditioning, but for the condition it created in those who roamed its fairways. Mention the back nine at Muny and people either laughed or shook their heads. The golf course was still a great bargain at just a few bucks for 18 holes. Whether you could walk those holes depended on how strong your heart was.

But we're skipping ahead. Golf had a strong history in the Capital District long before the Muny course earned its reputation. It's important to gain some historical insight before moving on.

Golf in the 1930s

Whether you're talking sports, politics, or infamous characters, 1931 was a hell of a year in Albany.

Franklin Roosevelt was in the Governor's Mansion, implementing statewide policies that would one day transform the country as the "New Deal." Albany's most bullet-friendly gangland figure, Jack "Legs" Diamond, was on trial just across the river for murdering a stubborn or stupid (or both) Greene County bootlegger by the name of Grover Parks. Albany's pride and joy, the Senators, were a hot item at Hawkins Stadium, having hosted a mid-summer exhibition with a couple of Yankee heroes named Ruth and Gehrig, and golf...golf was everywhere. On the front page, on the sports page and on the mind of the man who was about to give the capital city its first public golf course, Mayor John Boyd Thacher II.

While the country languished through the first years of the Great Depression, the sport of golf was capturing headlines around the country. America's first great links hero, Bobby Jones, was fresh from his unprecedented Grand Slam victory a year before. Jones swept the British Open, British Amateur, U.S. Open and U.S. Amateur, the latter by an amazing 8 and 7 score in the match play final.

The gentle Georgian was not only the country's greatest golfer, he also promoted the game with grace and good will. His twice-weekly newspaper columns on the sport, which ran in sports pages around the country, were as insightful and well written as anything before or since. In 1931, the man who would soon found the Augusta National Golf Club went Hollywood with a series of short instructional films. "How I Play Golf" ran for months at Albany's Strand Theater. Jones was, as

Tiger Woods has become, bigger than golf itself, and his persona drew thousands to the game.

Despite the dismal economy, Jones helped power a national obsession with the game. In 1930, an International News Service report counted 661,550 golfers holding club memberships in the United States, and that didn't take into account the growing number who were teeing off on the country's public and municipal links. "The largest number of golfers is found in New York," a news article on the report read, "its total being 63,149, or one in every 199 residents." Alabama apparently had the least interest in the game, with only one in 555 residents being a member of a golf club. Our New England neighbors to the east, Vermont (1 in 76 residents) and New Hampshire (1 in 45) had some of the highest ratios of golfers per capita in the country.

The 1920s and early 1930s were a time of steady growth for Capital District golfing, but none of the clubs saw the economic collapse to come.

Designed and built in the 1920s or early 1930s and shuttered for good by the Depression were several courses lost to the ages, although a few would later came back in different incarnations. Those that didn't included the Schalren Masonic Country Club, located picturesquely, as a *Times Union* article stated, "on the heights above the Mohawk River between Troy and Schenectady." Schalren opened in August 1930, and was called a "tricky and sporty set of holes," by local sportswriter Marty McDonagh. Later mention of the course in local newspapers becomes sparse and the club faded and failed, perhaps before the decade was out.

Also unable to sustain support were the Iroquois Golf Course in Niskayuna (which was used as an anti-tank training ground during World War II), and Schenectady Country Club. In Rensselaer County, Van Rensselaer Country Club, a popular 9-hole track, also faded into oblivion.

At Stop 13 ½ on the Troy-Schenectady Road, you would find Nippon Gardens, which opened there in 1930. As the name indicates,

Nippon Gardens was part nine-hole golf course, part intricate Japanese garden. But sports writers of the time describe it with far more color and without a hint of political correctness.

Writes the *Times Union* correspondent: Owner "P.M. Katow, a former Japanese subject, but for many years an adopted son of Troy, has put into the course all the artistry that goes with Jap gardening science. The atmosphere he has created is of a Japanese tea garden, with all the colorful trimmings. The course itself is not a miniature in any sense of the word, but a full man-sized course, where any golfer can get a kick out of hard driving, full-powered hip shots and his putting."

Hip shots? The course may have been located at the site of the current Mill Road Acres Golf Course, which is on the Troy-Schenectady Road (Route 7) and currently provides one of the best short-course layouts in the area.

Ghost courses came and went with the vagaries of the Depression, but those clubs that were able to hold on made do with reduced facilities and diminished coffers. The area's major private clubs survived and would live on to host continuing generations of golfing elite.

◆   ◆   ◆

The 1930s also saw the rise of the sportswriter whose summertime beat was primarily on the links (locally, most moved on to cover bowling in the winter). Golf writers, like all reporters, were a breed apart. On the Albany scene, the most familiar during the 1930s were Marty McDonagh of the *Times Union* and Ben Danforth of the *Knickerbocker Press.* Danforth went on to become the dean of local golf writers, with a career that lasted more than 35 years. He was instrumental in bringing the PGA Tour to the Capital District for its brief stay in the early 1950s (the Empire State Open was contested at Shaker Ridge and Normanside over a three-year period), and was known by his fellow reporters nationwide as an expert in the sport. Surprisingly, Danforth never took up what he often called "the old Scotch game."

In coverage, Danforth and McDonagh were nothing if not complete. A quick scan of local sports pages during the 1930s and 1940s shows some unusually comprehensive golf coverage. If you had a gross 93 for a net 71 at Mohawk or Albany or Edison, and topped your league, you wouldn't be stuck in agate type. You'd have a headline. Even a putting contest between two yokels merited a mention in McDonagh's "Tee-Talking it Over." Here's a sample:

"Wally Sharrett and Bill Potter met the other afternoon at the Edison Country Club in Schenectady on the putting green and after it was all over Potter was the winner. Sharrett paid for the dinners. Potter is a real divot digger and handles himself well on the green. Sharrett admits that he is not a champion. One wise cracker suggested they use shovels and baseballs next time."

Club championships drew preview stories and full coverage. Even the odd New York celebrity in town for the Saratoga racing meet would be mentioned, if he decided to take up a bag of clubs. As September began in 1931 and the horses retreated south, composer George Gershwin was spotted at McGregor Links with golfing notables Gene Sarazen and defending U.S. Open champ Johnny Farrell. The latter two were in town for the Glens Falls Open, which also drew tour regulars Billy Burke, Paul Runyan and Bobby Cruickshank. $3,500 in prize money was up for grabs.

Albany did have a truly legitimate national golf story in 1931. Tom Creavy, a short game wizard with an unassuming nature, had been named the new golf professional at Albany Country Club out on Western Avenue. Creavy may be considered a footnote in golfing history, but in 1931 he was a hometown hero. At age 20 and seven months, the Tuckahoe native became the second youngest golfer to capture the PGA Championship, defeating Denny Shute, 2 and 1, at Wannamoisett Country Club in Rhode Island. Only the charismatic Gene Sarazen, who Creavy swamped 5 and 4 in the '31 semifinals, was a younger champ, and that by a mere two months.

How stunning was the local pro's victory? Some 70 years later, the editors of *Golf* magazine were still calling it one of the top-10 surprises of the century in golfing. In a retrospective of Creavy's moment in the sun, *Sports Illustrated* golf writer Jaime Diaz praised the quiet phenom but also called him "the most obscure major champion of the modern era."

To be sure, Creavy was a first-rank professional but the national spotlight faded quickly following his lone PGA win. Perhaps he never wished for that spotlight in the first place. In addition to his teaching duties at Albany Country Club, Creavy continued to compete, making it through to the semifinals and quarters, respectively, at the PGA Championship the next two years. In 1934, he was one of a select group to play in the first Masters tournament. That same year, he won the San Francisco Match Play and tied the 18-hole scoring record at the U.S. Open, with a final round 66 at Merion. Just after that record mark, an accident in which he fell and injured his back all but finished his competitive playing days, but he continued to teach and mentor young golfers.

Creavy, whose brother Joe was a longtime pro at Colonie Country Club, finished out his career at the Saratoga Spa course and died of a heart attack in 1979. In an era when Watson and Nicklaus were dueling for dominance, Creavy's passing was a minor obit, but his legacy lives on, at least in the memory of local golfers who saw him play in his prime.

Ed Huba was 15 and the number one caddy at ACC when the new pro choose him to loop for a practice round. "He had just hitchhiked in from the West Coast. We went out on a cold April day. I still say he was the best pure hitter—the greatest shotmaker I ever saw," Huba said.

Tom Delaney, who followed Huba into the caddy ranks at Albany Country Club, said his introduction to golf was watching Creavy hit practice shots. The Delaneys had just moved to Albany from Syracuse and they heard there was some money to be made caddying at the country club just up the road from their house on the corner of Magazine Street and Western Avenue.

"I remember going up there that first day with my brother," Tom remembered. "Came up the road and there was this guy, hitting. It was Creavy, but we didn't know it. If he ever knew we up there looking to be caddies, he would of killed us. We were just sitting there watching him and our mother had us dressed up, so he must have thought we were member's kids. You'd put him up against any of the golfers today, even Freddie Couples, and I'd still say he was just as smooth."

"A wonderful guy, friendly," remembers Jack Vogel. "He was tall and slim, if you want the ideal golfer, that's what you want to start with—a tall, slim, wiry guy. Look at Tiger. What got to him was that he had spinal meningitis, and also, I heard this second hand and I can't remember from who, he was playing in a big tournament slipped on a tile floor in spikes and hurt his back. Never really the same player after that. But he was a beautiful golf player, a beautiful swinger."

Local duffers should be proud of the quiet PGA champ's relationship to the area. He remains the only pro associated with a local course to win one of golf's major championships.

With the muni courses gradually helping to make golf a workingman's sport and the post-WWII boom yet to come, golfers in the 1930s turned indoors for a time in the hopes of honing their skills. Little more than memories exist now, but for a brief 18 months Albany was one of the centers of the country's first miniature golf craze.

"Pygmy Golf" Comes To Albany

The first three years of the 1930s brought what can only be described as a "mini-golf mania" across the country. For a brief window of time, "pygmy golf" was a certified leisure-time craze, the last of the great fads of the 1920s, and probably one of the saner ones, when you consider the others included flag-pole sitting and swallowing goldfish. Albany even became a hub of putt-putt action nationwide, when the Institute for Golf and Recreation, an industry-wide trade group, was formed here in 1930.

Courses cropped up all over the Capital District and several even hired professionals to instruct and oversee the facilities. The set-ups were often lavishly decorated and included lounges and viewing areas to watch the action.

Take these lines from a *Times Union* article in November 1930:

> "Albany has granted numerous permits for indoor golf course this season. Almost 20 already are operating. Stores in undesirable locations, vacant buildings, such as sections of the Lyon block with huge garages, have been redecorated and rebuilt at outlays running to $12,000.
>
> "The construction has furnished employment to many men and has provided a new outlet for the entertainment money of Albany's public.
>
> "As early as July, when the miniature golf course was in the infancy of its popularity, there were in this country 5,846 of these midget links, all of which had settled themselves down to doing business on heretofore idle real estate. On August 11, according to figures announced by the department of commerce, there were

more than 25,000 pigmy courses in operation. The prediction by
many that the game would prove a fleeting fancy are unheeded by
those in the business."

Regrettably, those predictions were right on the money. Within a
year or two, miniature golf had begun to fade from the public consciousness, although several had tried adding driving nets to let golfers
take a full swing. As the decade wound out, the Depression put a scis-
sor-lock on the fad's future. An evening out to putt on carpet in a cav-
ernous warehouse became more luxury than the average man could
afford. The courses thinned and all closed within several years.

Another leisure time industry based out in Hollywood had a part in
mini-golf's demise. Since millions were choosing to play putt-putt
instead of visit the movies, film industry trade groups did everything
they could to block the expansion of miniature golf, fighting new
courses and thwarting groups who hoped to see the sport expand.

Miniature golf would not make a strong return to the national scene
again until the 1950s, and by then developers had figured that even the
putt putt variety of the game was best played outdoors.

Here's a partial list of the indoor golf courses operating in 1930 just
in the city of Albany and its immediate surroundings. In all, more than
20 courses were in operation at one time or another during the height
of the craze.

• The Menands Indoor Country Club, located on the Albany Troy
  Road

• The Lyon Block Course, on Market Street

• Westland Golf Garden, 241 West Lawrence, at Madison Avenue

• Park Central Golf Course, 276 Central Avenue

• Florida Gardens, Central Avenue

- Tum-Tum Golf Course, 1024 Broadway. Pro Tom Hurley had "taught some of the famous movie stars how to putt" according to a *Times Union* article.

- Kenwood Pass-Time Golf Course, 600 South Pearl Street

- The Everglades Golf Club, 525-527 Broadway

- The Hall, Harmanus Bleecker Hall (operated by Jerry and Jimmy Dwyer, professionals at Wolferts Roost, Jerry, soon to be pro at Albany Muni)

- Arcade Indoor Course, the Arcade on Broadway

- Bill Dennin's Putting Green, on Hudson Avenue

It's an odd moment in sports history—a brief country-wide fascination with putting ball to hole. Newspapers of the time, including the *Times Union* and *Knickerbocker News*, gave several inches of copy each day to the league results at Tum-Tum Golf Course way out on Broadway, or to those faithful Albany links junkies who played the Tuesday night winter league at the Lyon Block course. Perhaps it was the shared cultural memory of long-ago Dutch "kolfers" who gathered for some winter putting and a glass of brandy in the bargain.

A 10-Minute History of Golf in the Capital District

It's difficult to condense more than 100 years of local golf history into a few pages, but to gain a perspective on where Albany Muny fits in the timeline we have to take a look at the whole picture—or at least the Reader's Digest version of it.

The development of golf in this area can roughly be separated into three phases—the early clubs that catered to a wealthy clientele looking for something to complement their riding lessons and fox hunts; the newer, but still generally private, clubs that cropped up in the 1920s and 1930s; and the "post-Palmer" bubble of mostly public courses that opened in the 1960s and 1970s.

For our story, another era is worth mentioning. During the years of the Great Depression, municipal golf courses in Schenectady, Amsterdam, Troy, and here along the banks of the Normanskill were constructed. In Albany, and probably at other courses, state or federal works programs that kept thousands employed during the Depression helped fund the construction.

◆   ◆   ◆

The big picture of golf's origins in America is bound up in controversy, but it's safe to say the game was a Scottish transplant and truly began to take hold in the last decades of the 19th century. Few golf historians agree on where the game was actually played first on American soil. The Saint Andrews Golf Club, in Yonkers, holds firm on its being the first documented golf club (and the longest continuously operating), but courses in West Virginia, South Carolina, Pennsylvania and even South Dakota, may have pre-dated it. The United States Golf Association recognizes a much earlier incarnation, the South Carolina Golf Club, founded in 1786 in Charleston, South Carolina.

Our area's first golf "country club," according to "*The Architects of Golf*," a reference guide by course architect Geoffrey Cornish, was Albany Country Club, established in 1890. The course's original site was out Western Avenue, near the current site of the University at Albany. Van Schaick Island in Cohoes (which boasts the longest lineage at the same location), the Saratoga Golf and Polo Club, Mohawk in Schenectady and others soon followed near the turn of the century.

One of the most prominent early names in American golf architecture was responsible for several of the fledgling courses in this area. Devereux Emmet's name may not have the cachet of Donald Ross or A.W. Tillinghast, but his surviving courses are scattered throughout the eastern half of the country.

A descendant of one of America's wealthiest families, Emmet plied his trade in the first three decades of the century. The native New Yorker was the prototype rich guy who had the comfort and cash to do as he pleased. He golfed, hunted, raised dogs, traveled, and designed some 200 courses, many of his early tracts without charge. Emmet designed parts of Cherry Valley and private layouts for industrial giant Henry Dupont and the Vanderbilts. His most famous work is the Blue Course at Congressional Country Club, outside Washington, D.C., but his legacy in the Capital District is perhaps stronger than anywhere else in the country.

At age 29, Emmet was contracted to build the first Albany Country Club course, and in the coming years he also was to design Schuyler Meadows, Edison, McGregor, Mechanicville, Mohawk and the now defunct Schenectady Country Club. It's true that several of those courses have been greatly revised or tinkered by later hands, but Emmet was the originator.

Here's a brief rundown on the area's courses, the date they were established and the course designer. Some courses listed are no longer in business, but an effort was made to discover when and where they were. An excellent reference to all of the area's courses can be found in Dr. Douglas A. Lonnstrom's *Golf Courses of the Capital District*, published in 1998. *The Architects of Golf*, by Geoffrey Cornish and Ronald Whitten is an exhaustive compendium of all the courses constructed around the globe.

Early Clubs 1890-1925—As you might think for a game that takes money, acres of land and constant maintenance, the Capital District's early clubs were private and pricey. The type that would join a country club near the turn of the century was old blood and old money, Protestant and probably listed in the Blue Book, every city's guide to the social elite. As you can tell from the list below, Emmet's impact on the area's early golfing landscape is evident, although the renowned A.W. Tillinghast was called upon for Wolferts Roost, and Donald Ross marked his imprint on Glens Falls Country Club. Seymour Dunn, another name from the early days of golf architecture, had a special affinity for the mountains. He had a hand in many of the early courses constructed in the Adirondacks (Craig Wood, Lake Placid Resort, Saranac Inn, Ticonderoga CC).

No early history of golf in the Capital District, however brief, should leave out the impact of Arthur Knight of Schenectady, whose turn of the century tinkering led to one of the first major revolutions in club design. Knight was a GE engineer, Mohawk Golf Club member and part-time inventor. Casting club heads in a back yard shed, Knight designed a mallet headed, center-shafted putter and started using it at his home club in 1902. A year later, with modest yet full-scale production of the club begun, the putter ended up in the hands of America's leading amateur, Walter Travis. Fresh off top finishes in the 1902 US Open and 1903 US Amateur, Travis took the "Schenectady Putter" with him to England in 1904 where he became the first American to win the British Amateur title. Apparently, the Brits didn't take too kindly to the American's new contraption and several years later the Royal & Ancient banned all center-shafted clubs. That ban lasted another 40 years, but Knight's place in history had been secured.

Two of the area's most prominent courses—Albany Country Club and Colonie Country Club—were eventually engulfed by the march of progress and moved elsewhere. Albany's former location was on land now occupied by the University at Albany on Washington Avenue. In 1963, the club went to the New York State Supreme Court to contest the state's purchase price for the property. The club wanted $5 million for the 170-acre parcel, but the state's price was $2 million. They settled at $3.6 million, partly based on the expert testimony of the club's main witness, the eminent course architect Robert Trent Jones. Jones was already on retainer to design the club's new track in New Scotland. Colonie Country Club originally was located on the corner of Wolf Road and Central Avenue—the site of today's Colonie Center. It also relocated to New Scotland but retained the same name.

Albany Country Club/1890/Devereux Emmet, later relocated,
    redesign Robert Trent Jones Sr.
The Antlers Club/1925/Seymour Dunn
Columbia Golf and Country Club/1920/Hal Purdy
Colonie Country Club/1913/unknown, redesign Geoffrey Cornish
The Edison Club/1904/Devereux Emmet
Glens Falls Country Club/1912/Donald Ross
Hoosick Falls Country Club/1910/Club members
McGregor Links/1921/Devereux Emmet
Mechanicville Golf Club/1909/Devereux Emmet
Mohawk Golf Club/1898/Devereux Emmet
Saratoga Golf and Polo Club/1896/Unknown
Schenectady Country Club/Unknown/Devereux Emmet (NLE)
Van Schiack Island Country Club/1900/Club members
Wolferts Roost/1915/A.W. Tillinghast

Early Boom 1925-1940—Bobby Jones, bootleg liquor and boom times marked the 1920s, an era that saw another surge in the number of golf courses constructed around the country. The Great Depression put a damper on golfing worldwide but as you'll see from the list below, golf course construction continued through the 1930s in the Capital District. James Thompson, a teaching professional at Mohawk, excelled at creating functional and fun designs for the recreational golfer. Shaker Ridge, Western Turnpike and Schenectady Muni are three good examples. Not all course designs were masterpieces of form and function, but locals did what they could with the landscape available. Troy Country Club Superintendent John Melville was given the task of carving nine holes in city-owned Frear Park. A year later, Albany Mayor John Boyd Thacher asked Melville to tackle the swales along the Normanskill, and the original Albany Municipal Golf Course was born. During the waning years of the Depression, one big name course designer visited the area. Robert Trent Jones claimed Amsterdam Municipal as one of his first publicly funded layouts, in 1938.

Several courses constructed during the era couldn't swim through the economic turmoil and eventually closed shop. A few, such as Silver Brook, were partially reclaimed in later decades. Here's another example of the march of economic progress: The Stanford Golf Course was located on the site of one of the area's first shopping centers, Mohawk Mall, which eventually folded just 40 years after its construction. And another footnote to history—"Hap" Duval, grandfather of PGA pro David Duval served as pro of the Stanford club.

Albany Municipal Golf Course/1931/John Melville
Amsterdam Municipal Golf Course/1938/Robert Trent Jones Sr.
Ballston Spa Country Club/1926/James Thompson,
    additions Gino Turchi
Burden Lake Country Club (Totem Lodge)/1925/Unknown
Catskill Golf Club/1929/James Thompson
Cobleskill Golf and Country Club/1929/Unknown

Country Club of Troy/1926/Walter Travis
Frear Park Golf Course/1931/John Melville,
    back nine Robert Trent Jones Sr.
Iroquois Country Club/1920s/Unknown (NLE)
Normanside Country Club/1927/William Harries
Schenectady Municipal Golf Course/1935/James Thompson
Schalren Masonic Golf Course/1920s/Unknown (NLE)
Stanford Golf Club/1920s/Unknown (NLE)
Shaker Ridge Country Club/1931/James Thompson
The Sagamore/1928/Donald Ross
Schuyler Meadows Club/1927/Devereux Emmet
Silver Brook Country Club/1931/Walden Brough (NLE)
Van Rensselaer Country Club/1920s/Unknown
Western Turnpike Golf Course/1932/James Thompson

Post-Palmer Boom 1960-1980—With World War II safely behind us and the suburban explosion in full swing, a growing number of Americans suddenly had two important resources—money and leisure time. In the 1950s, however, golf was still seen by most as a rich person's game. The vast majority of clubs in the area were "members only," and youngsters hoping to give the game a shot did so by becoming caddies at the private clubs. Our president in the 1950s, Dwight Eisenhower, was an unabashed golf fanatic, but who could really relate to the man who conquered Hitler and then had to be coaxed into leading the free world? The national perception of golf started to change however when a young Pennsylvanian made his appearance on the shaky black and white image of the country's TV screen. With tree trunk arms, Arnold Palmer looked like an athlete and played golf as if it were gladiatorial combat. His victories were guts or glory affairs and his defeats were often equally dramatic. Simply put, he made golf "cool" for the average Joe.

Throughout the 1960s and early 1970s, Palmer's influence, coupled with the emergence of a guy named Nicklaus, fueled a steadily growing popularity of the sport. Golf courses, many of them public, began opening to players hungry for access but unwilling or unable to join a country club. Locally, entrepreneurs and landowners decided to try their hand at course design and the results were generally quite positive. Armond Farina and Gino Turchi led the bunch. Both accomplished golfers, (Farina was the pro at Schenectady Muni and Turchi a top-notch amateur) they invariably created courses that were fun and challenging for the average golfer, including two in Saratoga County—Northway Heights and Van Patten. Although not a local, course designer William Mitchell was responsible for several area layouts during the 1960s. Mitchell's work runs from the mundane to the masterful (Saratoga Spa State Course).

Frank Duane, who started out as an assistant to Robert Trent Jones Sr. in 1945, laid out two under-appreciated gems—the long-lost Tall Timbers, in New Scotland, and Sycamore, in Ravena—after breaking with RTJ in 1963. Duane was also responsible for another outstanding public track downstate. Spook Rock Golf Course is often listed as one of the top public courses in the country.

The Palmer era also saw the rise of two new distinctive golf layouts that would open the game to an even greater number of newcomers—the executive course, which could include a mixture of short par 3 and par 4s, and the par-3 course. Several examples are mentioned below.

Evergreen Country Club (nee Cordial Greens)/1960/Ed Van Kappen
Colonial Acres/1964/James Michaels
Eagle Crest (Northway Heights)/1963/Gino Turchi
French's Hollow/1968/John Betlejeski
Hiawatha Trails/1968/Dominic Ferraioli
Meadowgreens/1965/Unknown
Mill Road Acres/1974/Clayton Russell
Pinehaven Country Club/1960/Armond Farina
Riverview Country Club/1965/William Mitchell
Saratoga Spa Golf Course/1962/William Mitchell
Stadium Golf Course/1975/Douglas Hennel

Sycamore Country Club/1973/Frank Duane
Tall Timbers/1967/Frank Duane
Town of Colonie Golf Course/1969/William Mitchell/additional 9s
    Robert Trent Jones, Rick Jacobsen
Winding Brook Country Club/1960/Paul Roth (possible redesign of
    former Silver Brook Country Club)
Van Patten Golf Course/1969/Armond Farina

Mayor Thacher: Father of Albany Muny

Most of us could identify with John Boyd Thacher II on one count, at least. Sure, he was rich, powerful, graduated from the one of the country's top universities and held the mayor's office in the city of Albany for nearly a decade and a half. But on top of all that, he was a certified golf nut and a genuine lover of sports.

What other mayor would announce to an assemblage of newspaper reporters in March 1931 that the greatest satisfaction from a recent vacation was, "breaking 90 for the first time," and "playing 36 holes of golf every day." Thacher didn't even mention that one of his Florida foursomes, at St. Petersburg's Jungle Club, included Babe Ruth.

Mayor Thacher's 14 years (1927-1940) in office came during one of the greatest economic declines in American history, but he worked diligently to keep Albany's population above water. Overshadowed by the record-setting career of his successor, Erastus Corning, Thacher was the longest-serving Albany mayor to that point. In many ways, he was the model on which Corning was built.

Respectable, Protestant, intelligent, and heir to a political family that had already sent two to the Albany mayoralty, Thacher was the perfect candidate for the Democratic machine, a WASP to fly for the Irish bosses. Like Corning, he was patrician, popular and came from Albany's "Old Money." The Thachers ran one of the Northeast's largest wheel-making factories, the Cornings owned a railroad. The Thachers golfed at Albany Country Club, the Cornings preferred Schuyler Meadows.

Despite his highbrow credentials, Thacher's chief legacy as a mayor was in bringing widespread recreational activities to the youth of the city. Under his leadership, supervised summer programs were organized, public swimming pools built, and municipal playgrounds developed. Children may have been poor during the Depression, but in Albany at least, they had something to keep them busy.

During the mayor's term, Bleecker Stadium was built as a federal works project. The same year the Albany Municipal Golf course was opened, the Lincoln Park swimming pool, then one of the largest in the country, was opened to the public. Football fields were laid out at Tivoli Park, baseball diamonds blossomed in Sheridan Park and tennis courts were constructed at Linn Park under the mayor's direction.

Thacher is credited with bringing organized ice hockey to the city, and as a member of the Varsity Club, he was instrumental in creating Camp Thacher, a summer day camp for city children. He also helped organize the Central Boys Club on Sherman Street, which was the forerunner of the Albany Boys Club.

John Boyd Thacher II was born in Leadville, Colorado, in 1882. His parents had joined a prospecting boom that brought thousands to seek their fortune in the West's newly discovered deposits. Thacher's father, George Hornell Thacher, was the son of Albany's 50th mayor, also named George Hornell Thacher, and nephew to mayor number 57, JBT II's namesake, John Boyd Thacher I.

The original JBT was an interesting figure, not only a mayor and manufacturer but also one of the greatest Christopher Columbus scholars of his time. His collection of research material is housed at the Library of Congress and includes original manuscripts, autographs and other printed materials from the Age of Exploration through the French Revolution. "He had quite an outstanding collection," said Jack McEneny, a state Assemblyman and former city historian, who's reviewed the collection. "I think at the time it was considered the most important collection of its kind."

While the scholarly John Boyd was poring over manuscripts and writing biographies of Columbus and John Cabot, his nephew George was learning the game of golf, and eventually passing it down to his son, the future mayor. George Hornell Thacher was one of the founders of the Ekwanok Country Club in Manchester, Vt., and photos passed down through the family show him in a foursome that included President William Howard Taft and Abraham Lincoln's son, Robert Todd. "We have a lot of old photos of George Hornell Thacher at Ekwanok," said Betty Thacher, a niece of the mayor. "He must have passed on his love of golf to his son."

After Colorado, the Thacher family settled back in Albany, where JB was schooled at Albany Academy for Boys. He received a degree at Princeton, and then returned to his hometown to study at Albany Law School. Thacher was admitted to the bar in 1906, but instead of jumping into practice, he worked in the family business until his father's death in 1929. By then, he had already secured a growing reputation among the city's Democratic leadership.

Thacher's interest in politics was probably in-born and fostered in the belief that he was carrying on a noble family tradition. He was, as newspaper accounts attest, an agreeable gentleman and an extremely fine speaker. A tall figure with a stentorian voice, he made his reputation in 1930 by delivering a ringing speech at the state convention supporting Presidential candidate Al Smith, then the state's governor. But for all his oratory skill, intelligence and charm, Thacher had the look of a wizened college professor rather than a big city mayor.

Despite his bookish appearance, the mayor was an extremely popular leader, racking up increasingly large pluralities in his four election runs. Two years after his convention speech, he himself came a hair's breadth away from the governor's chair. Upstate Democrats were touting Thacher for the governorship, but he eventually bowed to Roosevelt's lieutenant governor, Herbert Lehman, who served in the Capitol nearly as long as Thacher remained Albany's mayor.

The mayor's four consecutive terms spanned the waning days of the Roaring 20s and the dark economic period that lasted until the beginning of the 1940s. While, in general, the Northeast was not as hard hit as other areas of the country, unemployment rose, banks defaulted and much of the industry that fueled the economy slowed to a crawl.

By the end of his first term, Mayor Thacher had already begun considering ways to bring more jobs to the working men and women of Albany. Then-Governor Franklin D. Roosevelt had some ideas of his own. Working with local and municipal officials, Roosevelt began formulating, at a statewide level, "Emergency Work Relief Projects," programs that came to be known as The New Deal.

With a combination of state and local funds, projects that employed thousands were being created across New York, and just outside the city limits of Albany, a stretch of hilly ravine along the banks of the Normanskill was selected for a unique purpose. Mayor Thacher was planning to bring his love of golf to the men, women and children of Albany.

In years to come, golfers would contest for the John B. Thacher Trophy (later the Corning Trophy), the symbol of the Albany city championship. He himself would play in charity events at the course and contend against caddies, professionals and statesmen alike. The mayor had made the course, now he was going to enjoy it.

A Golf Course is Born

By 1929, the idea of a municipal golf course for the people of Albany had already been brewing in the mind of Mayor Thacher for several years. With dozens of recreational initiatives for the city's young people underway, the new mayor turned his focus to the city's adult population. Golf obviously was one of Thacher's favorite pastimes; with a little funding and the right piece of land he hoped to introduce city residents—from bricklayer to banker—to the game.

But with the Great Depression beginning its decade-long stranglehold on the national economy, that funding was tight. Thacher answered the call of fellow Democrat, Governor Franklin Roosevelt, who in 1929 was urging New York's mayors to create municipal works projects that would provide needed jobs for working men and women hard hit by the economic downturn. These efforts at the statewide level were the genesis of projects Roosevelt would later implement nationwide as the New Deal. In the mayor's eyes, however, the new golf facility wasn't much of a risk. He was convinced that, after the initial financial outlay, a public golf course would be self-sustaining.

There may have been a little municipal jealousy at work in the mayor's plans as well. By mid-1930, Troy's Parks and Recreation department had announced its plan to build a golf course at the city's Frear Park. While Schenectady, the other tri-city, would not build a municipal links for another five years, it must have galled Thacher that the Trojans were beating him to the punch. He was, after all, building a reputation as the mayor who would bring recreation to the people.

In his annual Mayor's Message of 1929, Thacher hinted at his plans:

"As part of the park program and in connection with the recreational facilities of the city of Albany, the development of a municipal golf links is an important consideration," he wrote, and concluded, "The popularity of this game, together with the growing interest on the part of the public generally in this form of exercise make it imperative that such a course be established…"

Like almost all things in government, the project started with a committee, a brain trust of movers and shakers who could figure out the financing, choose the site, hire an architect and raise support. Chairing the committee was Alfred Sporborg, a friend of the mayor and president of Steefel Brothers Inc. Joining him were Jacob Herzog, vice president of the National Commercial Bank and Trust Company; John H. McElroy, secretary of the Consolidated Car Heating Company; George I. Lawyer, a local businessman and fellow Schuyler Meadows golfer; and Frederick Futterer, Thacher's aide in all public projects dealing with recreation in the city.

The committee met throughout the later half of 1929, and although the process has been lost to history, they eventually decided on a 262-acre parcel of land just beyond the city line on New Scotland Avenue, in the town of Bethlehem. With other, more desirable areas undeveloped on the western edge of the city, it's questionable why the Normanskill tract was chosen. Perhaps it was money. Perhaps the committee didn't want to build too closely to the Albany Country Club site on Washington Avenue.

More likely, they wanted an area that was more accessible to the men and women who would frequent the new muny links. In 1930, the ride out Washington or Western Avenue wasn't a quick drive in your automobile. It was a trip via Albany Transit or car that may have taken 30 minutes; not the kind of spot to reach easily for a second shift machinist or a teenage caddy. They needed someplace accessible by public transportation and they needed a ready seller. They apparently found both on the rolling farmlands of Al Walley and Peter O'Neil.

Although 262 acres was more than enough to build an 18-hole course (the mayor had initially planned two 18s), several parcels of land were eyed for the course and what he hoped would become a nature park along the Normanskill. The final price for the total 262-acre parcel was less than $150,000.

While accessible, the committee's choice of land would prove to be a challenge for any golf course architect. Across the Normanskill in 1927, a landscape contractor and fledgling golf course designer by the name of William Harries had carved 18 holes around the ravines and rolling hills of the Salisbury farm. But at Normanside Country Club, Harries skirted the sharp contours of the land when he could, and integrated the slopes into par threes and long downhill par fours.

On the Albany side of the creek however, the ravines were steeper and closer together. Who could build a golf course among these wooded hills? Lacking the money to bring in a professional course architect, the Albany committee turned to the man who had laid out Troy's recent nine at Frear Park—John Melville, the Troy Country Club Superintendent. Melville's name does not appear in "The Architects of Golf," the encyclopedia of nearly every course built around the world, and it's unlikely that his prior experience went beyond the Troy nine he helped develop. His selection seems to be based on his availability and the knowledge he gained at Frear.

In 1930, while also working on the Troy course, Melville laid out a rough and temporary nine-hole track in the open area available off New Scotland. Thacher and the committee were elated when more than 15,000 showed up that summer to test out the new nine, which was opened to the public for free.

Work on the official Albany Municipal Golf Course began in May 1931, with rough grading and clearing brush and trees from the proposed layout. Of the 262 acres, six acres were orchard, another six were woodland and the remainder considered farm or pasture land.

While work began on the 18-hole course, play continued on the temporary nine. Between mid-June and September, an amazing 20,000 residents and visitors registered to give the course a shot. No matter what Melville provided, the new course at Albany seemed destined for success. Newspaper reports were noting that the temporary course was seeing an average 200 players a day. "From shortly after sunrise until twilight, the links are dotted with embryo Bobby Joneses and the usual large flock of duffers. Saturday and Sunday the lineup at the start is usually 30 or 40 deep," one account noted.

By September, the fairways were ready for their final top dressing—100 pounds per acre of fescue, Kentucky blue grass and Red Top. The temporary 18 holes were closed to the public and the grass allowed to take root. The final price tag for the new Albany Municipal Golf Course was a mere $70,402.40.

The course was a budgetary success, but quite obviously not a work of art. For some reason, Melville had decided to design several holes across the landscape's gaping valleys and ravines. At holes 6, 7, 8, 12, 13 and 15, stairs were constructed so that golfers could negotiate the hills. It was the beginning of the course's reputation. You had to be a billy goat to play at Albany Muni. "It's certainly the sportiest I've ever played and it is no place for weak knees, sister!," commented one unnamed player interviewed by a reporter. "A Rocky Mountain goat would be winded if he chased around that near nine."

Although the mayor had held an "opening drive" ceremony on the first nine holes in May of 1931, a year later he officially dedicated the Albany Municipal Golf Course on May 28, 1932. Thacher gave a few waggles and let loose with what one newspaper columnist called a "screaming 200 yards drive." Thacher was out in 45 and came home in 44 on the par 72 course. More importantly, he beat the rest of his foursome, which included Melville, Sporborg and Deputy Public Works Commissioner Alfred Schlosser, who oversaw the course construction.

Youngsters came from around the city to carry bags or get the chance to test the new course out for themselves. Some played a few times and lost interest; others grew to love the game. "We were all caddies at Albany Country Club but we would go over to muny even before the old clubhouse was built," said Robert Huba. "We could play all day for 50 cents, sometimes we just played and played until it got dark. It was hilly but we didn't mind it. We got to love the game. It was our course."

Teeing off at the first hole, circa 1938. Note caddy at right, ready to loop another 18. *Courtesy of the Albany County Hall of Records*

One of the numerous bridges constructed to help golfers climb the Muny hills. *Courtesy of the Albany County Hall of Records*

This may have been the course's caddyshack, which burned down in the late 1930s. The orchard in the back may have been part of the Walley Farm. *Courtesy of the Albany County Hall of Records*

The old clubhouse in its glory years. *Courtesy of the Albany County Hall of Records*

Construction of the original course. The final price tag was just over $70,000. *Courtesy of the Albany County Hall of Records*

The view from the original 11th green, looking back toward the clubhouse, in the late 1930s. The 11th would later become the 12th and be shortened to a par 4. *Courtesy of the Albany County Hall of Records*

Joe Ruszas, a Muny caddy in the 1930s who went on to win the New York State Amateur title. Note the caddy badge clipped to his belt. *Courtesy of Ginny Ruszas*

In later years, Joe Ruszas (in white Hogan cap) would briefly serve as head pro at Shaker Ridge Country Club and also compete in many charity events. The reporter in the middle may be a very young Howard Tupper. *Courtesy of Ginny Ruszas*

Ed Huba, at right, shows off the form that won him the Times Union Hole-in-One contest one year. Third from the left is the old pro himself, Jerry Dwyer. *Courtesy of Ed Huba*

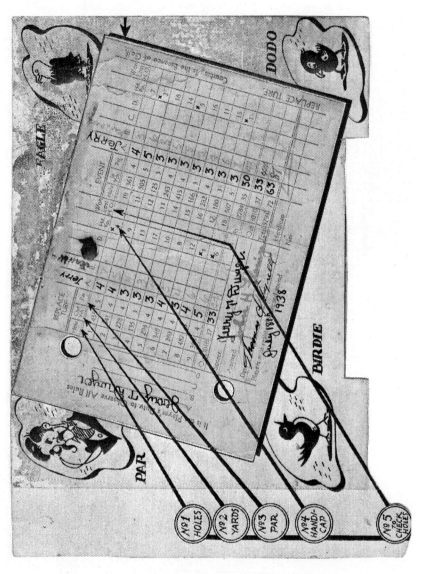

Jerry Dwyer's record scorecard from 1938. Eight birdies and one eagle led to a then record round of 63, nine under par. *Courtesy of Gerry Zwack*

Jerry Dwyer showing off his form in later years. *Courtesy of Gerry Zwack*

Muny's NENYPGA junior interclub champs from 1962. The team was sponsored by the Oppenheim VFW Post. Kneeling from left, Richie Maxstadt, Howard Schulman, Charlie Murphy and Mike Daniels. Standing, Bob Smith, Mike Bloom, Harold Menchel and coach/manager Clem McMahon. *Courtesy of Charles Murphy*

The 1930s

The course's first decade was noteworthy for its success. That first full year (1932), the course totaled more than 28,000 registered players, and the city estimated that the average number of rounds for a season pass holder was 33.

Albany Municipal, or simply "Muny" as it was later called, fit a Depression-era pocket as well. The single round fee of 50 cents was to last for at least another 15 years, and few golf diehards, if they had the lung capacity, stopped at just 18 holes. More than one young golfer remembers playing literally sun-up to sundown.

Through the first 10 years at Albany, city records show the yearly total of registered golfers at around 35,000, very respectable when you consider that the economic downturn was followed by a war that took many of the city's able-bodied golfers.

In the later part of the 1930s, Albany Common Council minutes noted several additions that mysteriously never came to fruition. In 1937, the council authorized a WPA project for a new nine-hole course, as well as funding for four tennis courts. $300,000 in bonds were authorized for the work, but neither the nine-hole course nor the tennis courts were ever built. Another similar ordinance came through the Common Council in 1938, when the tennis courts were finally completed. In the mayor's annual message that year, Thacher noted that "two new badminton courts and three tennis courts were built on the Municipal Golf Course (property), while considerable work was done on the construction of an additional nine-hole golf course."

What became of the new nine-hole course, or the badminton courts for that matter, is not known. A year later, the mayor came up with a truly practical project for the WPA workers—new wooden stairways across some of the fairways.

1937 was a banner year at the course. During the summer, the muny hosted an exhibition featuring a quartet of the top professionals in the game. Sporting goods manufacturer Spalding corralled Harry Cooper, Lawson Little, Masters champ Horton Smith, and long-hitting Jimmy Thomson, (the John Daly of his day) to barnstorm the nation by train, offering clinics and exhibitions. Albany Muny was one of their first stops, and hundreds turned out to follow the foursome as they attacked the municipal layout. (A picture of the golfers can be seen hanging on the wall at Beffs restaurant bar in Delmar.)

During the 1930s, the course was to see its first three-time champion in Frank Cummings and the rise of several other prominent golfers who went on to vie for local and state amateur titles.

Frank Cummings

The trophy was three feet tall, the younger Frank Cummings said. Somewhere along the line, it simply disappeared. Frank lives in Albany and plays golf every now and then. His father, the senior Francis Cummings, was a bit more serious about the game. In the 1930s, Cummings was the first to become a three-time winner of the Mayor Thacher Trophy, a feat that would be accomplished by only four other golfers throughout the years.

"It was a big trophy, I remember, but it's probably long gone by now," said the son. Cummings Sr. pulled off the feat in three consecutive years—1933 through 1935—but he and his twin brother, John, would remain competitive throughout the 1930s in the Mayor's Cup tournament that would soon be considered the muny's annual championship.

In 1938, John Cummings was involved in the only disputed tournament final on record, although the story is a bit second hand. Jack Vogel, a generation younger than the Cummings twins and a student of the game himself, was compiling a list of past city champions in the late 1950s. He wanted some recognition for those who had won the city title and, finding the clubhouse bar empty of such, he set out to comb the newspapers. "I asked Mickey Marcy. I said 'If I can get these all together, would you put up a plaque or something?' So I started working on the list. The only year that I couldn't find was this one—1938. John Cummings and Clare Graves played in the final, and I asked Jerry Dwyer about it and he said there was no winner. I can't remember exactly what he said happened, but there was some kind of penalty called and they never resolved it," Vogel said.

Frank was a CBA grad, class of 1925. He worked for the telephone company most of his life, retiring in 1971. The three-time champion married later in life so his younger years were often spent around the golf course. Marriage came and the golf became secondary. His son remembers his father telling him about playing on the tour for a while, and that's quite possible. To enter most tour events in those days all one needed was a handicap below two and the entrance fee. Money winners, of course, would have forsaken their amateur status.

"He tried to teach us when we were kids. We would go out to the old muny course or Western Turnpike," younger Frank said. "These days, I get out when I get a chance, maybe three or four times a year," said Frank. "I'm a typical hacker. I'll never get any better."

The Huba boys

In the back of Ed Huba's silver Ford Escort, he keeps a few carefully wrapped plastic bags. In these are newspaper clippings, photocopies of Common Council meeting minutes, and the occasional dog-eared picture from the mid-1950s—golfers standing around the muny target green located where today's ninth green sits. They are the reminders he keeps handy when he wants to prove a point or remember a fact. You see, Ed knows the course and the people who played there better than almost anyone. In 1932 (and it seems like yesterday to him), he was a kid, trudging with his brothers down to the newly opened muny.

Today, as he enters his late 80s, he still visits the course on a pretty regular basis.

Ed is a humble, self-effacing fellow who keeps stored away in his head the memories of nearly seventy years of golf at the muny.

Tell anyone who's spent a few years hanging around course that you're thinking of writing a book about the place. "Have you talked to Eddie Huba?" they'll ask. "He's got pictures. He knows everything about this place, absolutely everything."

More than a few pictures and old clippings, Ed has a passion for golf and, if I may assume, a soft spot for this series of swales and ravines formerly known as the Albany Municipal Golf Course. If you've played golf at the same club for 70 years, how can you not consider it your second home?

Decades ago, a friend called Ed and wanted to know how to play the muny course. Ed wrote out a brief description of the holes and an educated rundown on how to play them. Years later, when they were constructing what would become the New Course at Albany, Ed came down and took pictures, chatted with the archaeologists. His daughter jokes that, when the time comes, Ed will probably want his ashes scattered across the old course. Today, when he looks across the driving range, his eyes glint. He doesn't see the driving range, he sees what was there before it—the old ninth hole coming in and the old tenth going out. He points to a healthy stand of trees and remembers mere saplings. By default, if nothing else, Ed Huba is the unofficial historian of Albany Muny.

"Don't get to be 85 years old, the memories escape you," he says. "Some days I come out here and I sit and I can visualize what this place used to look like 70 years ago. It was nothing, except for a few cows."

The Huba boys, all seven brothers, climbed one by one into the caddy ranks, baptized into golf the only way working class kids were in those days. One of the older kids on Quail Street, Bill Tansy, had found work at the Albany Country Club and the Huba boys followed.

Joe, Harold, Walt, Ray, Ed, Al, and Bob all toted bags at the old ACC, and they learned the game from sheer persistence.

"With 10 kids, you moved around a lot. We lived out near Albany Country Club for a time—Homestead Street or it was called Stop 7. The church there was St. Margaret Mary's. So we only had to walk across the street," Ed remembers.

"You always had a club in your hand. If you got over the hill, you'd take a ball out of your pocket and hit it around and that's how you learned. Of course, when this municipal course opened, all the caddies started to play. We could afford the fee. It was fifty cents; and just ten dollars for the season. When I started caddying, it was just like the 1990s, there was prosperity, everything was going. It was the Roaring 20s. We would get a buck and a half. But when the 1930s came and the Depression, it went down to a buck, and you still had to give the caddymaster a dime. Then they dropped it down again, to 75 cents. Most of golfers gave you that extra quarter. Even so, you could be making half of what you made a few years back.

"The members would give us a few clubs and we'd learn a lot just by watching the better players. When they opened this course, we'd get down here as much as we could. Sometimes we were able to play 36 holes in one day."

The wooly patch of farmland that was being transformed into a golf course that summer of 1931 was more than a trolley ride south to New Scotland Avenue for Huba. It was the place he and brothers, among thousands of others, honed their fledgling golf games.

As they grew older, the younger Huba boys kept at the game, and their prowess on the links would become known across the region. After the war, Ray moved on to Normanside and then Pinehaven, where he collected more than a few trophies. He also became one of the most respected detectives in Albany's police department. Bob, likewise, joined Normanside and then Wolferts Roost. Al should have made Ripley's Believe it or Not by now. In a 40-year career at Western Turnpike, he won that course's championship a total of 21 times—the first time in 1948 and the last sometime in the late 1980s. That's got to be some kind of record.

Ed stayed on at the Muny. He played with his brothers when he could. He disdained the leagues that clogged the course in the late afternoon, and he enjoyed the company of a few choice foursomes. When you reach your eighties, however, foursomes have a way of thinning out. Ed's the only one left from his regular group.

He still drives from his Pine Hills home over to the course on a pretty regular schedule. In summer, Ed meets up with some friends who've been around the place for a few years. When the course is closed, he'll still be there for a walk around, if it's not too cold. He carries one of those adjustable golf clubs that, with the flip of a screw, can become any iron you'd like. "It's nice getting out here. I just hit the ball around a little bit, nothing much. It's nice to be able to swing the club, you know."

The Ruszas boys

Albany Municipal Golf Course has had a few homegrown heroes, but the first was probably Joe Ruszas, a Livingston Avenue kid with a sweet swing and the guts to face down a nearly crippling accident to win the State Amateur title in 1944.

All four of the Ruszas boys were golfers, Charlie, Joe, Al and Stanley, neighborhood boys rising through the caddy ranks at Muny and Wolferts Roost, honing their swings with hand-me-down clubs. Joe and Charlie were the prodigies, it seems; trading titles and accolades throughout the Capital District's amateur ranks during the 1930s and 40s.

Joe was a Muny bag-toter from the start, and he won one of the course's first caddy tournaments in 1932. Mayor Thacher, whose bags Joe carried on occasion, challenged the teenager to a match and was promptly whipped. The Mayor didn't stand a chance.

A machinist by trade, Joe racked up three city championships and at least two Albany County titles. Charlie added a city title to the family mantle a few years later. Through local qualifying, Joe made it to the State Amateur tournament at least three times. In 1943, he finished as runner-up to Ray Billows, a perennial power from the Binghamton area. Three years later, Ruszas would lose to Billows in the state tournament semi-finals. In 1944, however, Ruszas had all cylinders working. The 36-hole final needn't have gone to the second 18. Joe ended up winning 13 and 11, surely one of the most lopsided wins in state tournament history.

By the time he was vying for State Amateur titles, Joe was a member at Shaker Ridge Country Club and, beginning in 1946, he was briefly the pro at the course. Throughout the 1940s, he held the course records at Edison (62) and Troy Country Club (66).

For sure, all the Ruszas boys were top-flight amateurs, but what made Joe's story truly memorable was his recovery from a machine shop accident that nearly ended his playing career. Ruszas was in his 20s and working at Simmons Machine Tool in Menands when his left hand was mangled in the accident. He slowly recovered some motion in his wrist, but from then on, he had to adapt his swing to compensate for the injury. Within a few years, Ruszas was back amidst the area's top amateur golfers. Within five years, he had won the state amateur title.

Ruszas was to face several more battles that would test more than his mettle to play competitive golf. In his early thirties, he lost an eye to a form of melanoma, and at age 36 the cancer returned to claim his life.

Joe's daughter Ginny was only 12 years old when her father died in 1956. She remembers her father as "a very gentle, kind man."

"It's strange, some of the things you remember when you're that age. I remember him loving Jello with fruit cocktail," she said, smiling, "and I remember looking out the window on Livingston Avenue, seeing him standing in front of St. George's Church with his brothers."

Ginny has a few scrapbooks worth of newspaper clippings to keep her father's golfing exploits in memory. There are photos of Joe with Schenectady pro Armand Farina, playing in a charity match to benefit infantile paralysis; notes of him playing with Mayor Corning in another charity match, (one that drew more than 1,000 spectators to the muny course) and, of course, the *Knickerbocker News* articles announcing his state amateur win. For a few short years, the dapper Albany man was the toast of amateur golf, and among good company, considering the tough competition locally.

For all their golfing skill, those who remember the Ruszas family of golfers remember their style as much as their ability on the links.

"I don't know what it was about them, but they always looked good, dressed like a million bucks," said one contemporary. "I got the impression they were some kind of international playboys they way they dressed."

On and off the golf course, their personalities matched their game. Charlie was the "natural" and Joe the quiet, tireless technician. "Charlie was a great natural player, a natural swinger. But Joe was more of the technician, and he practiced," said Jack Vogel, who counts Charlie among his friends. "Charlie very seldom practiced. His practice was going out and playing, and yet he was able to maintain a good game. Charlie was a playboy, even as a kid."

The playboy kid grew up to be flesh and blood swell, the kind of vagabond sportsman whose life was a series of simple pleasures. "In this world there are spenders and there are makers. I happen to be a spender," he once told *Times Union* sports editor Tom Cunningham.

After a stint in the Navy, Charlie (who goes by Charlie Rush) headed south to Miami Beach, where he worked at two country clubs—Bay Shore and Normandy Isle. After 51 years in the golf game, he retired, better to concentrate on another consuming love—the ponies of Gulfstream race track. He comes up for the Saratoga meet, teaches the occasional lesson at Hoffman's driving range and seems to know everybody there is to know.

In a late 1970s column, Cunningham called Charlie "Albany's answer to Lee Trevino."

"Charlie would wager one and all that he could break 40 on the back nine at Muny using nothing but a mallet headed putter. It was no gamble. He was never higher than 38," Cunningham wrote. "With regulation golf sticks in hand, Rush played in the low 60s at Muni and went on to turn professional. But for the past 25 years or so, Charlie Rush has dedicated his life to having a good time."

"Look," Charlie told Cunningham. "I tried working and I didn't like it. I was the leading salesman for Brown and Bigelow nationwide at one time. I was a skilled machinist and I played in a few professional golf tournaments. But there is nothing like just doing what you want to do. Life is too short and when you go, you're worth about 15 cents in dust. Whatever you have in this world you are just borrowing because when you go, you can't take it with you."

The 1940s

By the beginning of the 1940s, Albany Muny was an unqualified financial success, but by the end of the decade, even the city fathers realized that the course needed some serious work. What they gave it was a low-cost makeover. In 1949, the course dumped its first two original holes (rerouting the first) and squeezed another par three into the back nine. The layout was shifted to move all of the hilly holes to the back nine, thus creating a legend and making the course a par 70, instead of its original par 72.

The 1940s saw the rise of several golfers who were to crowd the city championship during the decade, Joe Ruszas, Peter Van Kampen and Tom Delaney; even Ruszas' brother, Charlie, got in the act by taking the title in 1945. Joe Ruszas was a muni caddy during his youth and went on to serve briefly as a pro at Shaker Ridge. Delaney and Van Kampen were both former Albany Country Club caddies who fell in love with the game. Frank Hoeffner, who would go on to take the city title three times in the mid-1950s, also began his playing career as a youngster during the 1940s.

The war years were tough on golf courses across the country, depleting the supply of able-bodied duffers. According to several old-timers, men who had joined the service and were home on leave were able to play for free.

Frank Hoeffner

Talk to enough old Muny golfers and you'll hear the same stories—tales of the hills, the indoctrination of the game through the caddying ranks, boys who learned to love the game because, to them, it was just nice to be with their neighborhood chums swinging a club and chasing a ball. City kids in the 1930s and 1940s didn't get much opportunity to wander the open fields of a golf course

"It seemed nice to walk on the grass, to be outside," said Frank Hoeffner, with simple honesty. "The putting green was like a smooth carpet. And, of course, we were with our friends."

Hoeffner, who captured the Mayor Corning Cup (the city's championship) in 1954, 1955 and 1957, was an Arbor Hill kid who benefited from growing up in close proximity to Wolferts Roost Country Club, the well-manicured, A.W. Tillinghast layout in neighboring Loudonville. "We all caddied there," he recalled. "It was a way to get you off the street, and it got you some money."

Hoeffner and his buddies caught the golf bug toting clubs at the exclusive Roost, but their first sticks came from the Salvation Army on Clinton Avenue. Like the Scottish golfers of old, the Dudley Heights boys had piecemeal collections—a wood gathered here, a cast-off iron donated by a now forgotten country club duffer. Mostly, they settled for the hickory-shafted variety, which by the late 1930s was quickly fading from the club player's bag. A steel shafted iron or wood, on the rare occasion one turned up, became a prized possession.

Like the caddies at most private clubs, Hoeffner and friends had the chance to play 18 holes each Monday the course was closed. He made good use of those Mondays and also snuck in a few holes during the weekday evenings he could walk over to the club. "We were close to the pro out there, Jack Gormley, and the guys who ran the course. They would let us out after 6 to play a little," he said.

Hoeffner's game progressed through his teenage caddying years due, in part, to the ideal practice facility across the street from his home. Philip Livingston High School's wide expanse of lawn was a great place to pull out the clubs and hit shag balls, he said.

In his early 20s, he began frequenting the muny across town, taking the bus with clubs in tow or stashing them away in the locker room. In his late 20s, he captured the first of his three city championships, but, to him, it honestly, "was no big thing." The competition, perhaps, was secondary to the game itself, and the camaraderie that went along with it.

"I remember I played Lou Weinman in the finals one year. Sometimes they would have a good field, sometimes they wouldn't," he said.

With modesty, Hoeffner downplays his achievement. For the city finals, golfers had to qualify with one of the low 16 scores to make it into the match play championship flight. From there, they had to win four consecutive matches to take the cup. To do that three times within a four-year span is some accomplishment.

Pressed for details, the one-time city courts employee will talk awhile about the golfers he encountered out on the old course. In addition to his neighborhood pals, Richard Clark and Dan Tanski, a couple of Siena grads and fine golfers in their own right, Hoeffner vied against the muny's top golfers during one of its golden eras.

"Red" Williams, the city cop on disability who managed to negotiate the hills of Albany Muny every day, ("he lived at the course, a grand guy to play with...") was probably one of the most readily known figures at the old course. A motorcycle cop, Red was city champion in 1942 and nearly pulled off the same feat 17 years later when he was ousted twice in the finals by a new generation of golfers. Williams was so well known around the links that his obituary was headlined "J.F. Williams Dies; Albany's 'Golfing Cop'"

Jack Reilly, who also captured several city championships during the 1950s, was another likely rival of Hoeffner's among the Muny's top golfers.

Golfers who won the city championship three times were said to have "retired the cup." That meant the city ponied up enough money and bought a trophy you could take home for good. The names of the previous winners were etched on the side and from pictures, it looked like a pretty nice piece of hardware.

Hoeffner's trophy was "handled around a bit," he said, and, although not stated, you get the impression it eventually fell apart.

They gave him a replacement though, a wooden plaque that he said he could probably dig out if he looked around. "It's around here somewhere," he said.

Hoeffner played throughout the 1950s at the Muny but by the 1960s, he'd had enough of the hills. Eventually, he moved on to Ballston Spa Country Club and then McGregor Links, but for the lifelong city resident, the hikes up into Saratoga County got to be too much. These days, he visits the "new" course from time to time, but his competitive golfing days are in the past.

"The course was no gem, but you have to remember that this was about the only place to play if you weren't a member of a club," he said.

Tom Delaney

Around the same time Frank Hoeffner was beginning his bag-toting duties down at Wolferts Roost, Tom Delaney was winning his first caddy tournament up on Western Avenue at the old Albany Country Club. Delaney, another three-time Mayor's Cup winner, gets sentimental about the now gone Albany Country Club layout, a place he called "an absolutely gorgeous golf course."

"It was so rustic and natural. It had these beautiful pine trees," he said. "And when all the other courses were too wet to play, you could play there because it was all sand. It drained beautifully."

Growing up near the corner of Magazine Street and Western, Delaney was a mere stroll up the road from one of the area's premier country clubs. He learned the game through the caddying ranks, but also made full use of his proximity to the golfing home of Albany's elite.

Carrying bags for "lawyers, doctors, bankers and judges," was a learning experience of its own sort, but his Monday rounds were where he and his brother honed their games. "We would play the front course and then go to the back course. We'd be going around that place like nothing, sometimes 72 holes in one day, I'm not kiddin'. I was always playing when I could," he said.

Delaney isn't kidding. He's got sepia-toned pictures of his brother and he taking cuts on the old ACC course when there's still snow on the ground. They even had the implied consent of the guard who was there to chase non-members. When the guard, a disabled WWII veteran, found out one of Delaney's friends was a disabled vet, he used to run interference for the Magazine Street group.

Albany Muny was a good two miles across town but that didn't deter Delaney and the rest of the young uptown golfers. With bags on their back, they'd stroll down Krumkill Road for what usually turned out to be another marathon session on the links. "We'd walk over to Albany Muny, play all day and then walk back," Delaney said. "We would walk everywhere in those days."

Humility must infect these city champ golfers, because like Hoeffner, Tom Delaney isn't one to blow his own horn. He took the Albany Muny crown in 1946, 1947 and 1950, but if pressed he would rather talk about the time he watched Bobby Locke dismantle Troy Country Club or when he followed Hogan around a Catskills layout rather than any city title he ever won.

Delaney's memories of the club championships are hard to pull. In 1946, he and "Bucky" Minney played all square through the 36-hole final and Delaney topped him on the first extra hole. Three years later, he lost to another top muny golfer, Peter Van Kampen. Topping Richie Clarke, 7 and 5, in the 1950 title match, Delaney built a substantial five-hole lead with a hot morning round of 68.

Although they often drew crowds out of the bar as they came up the 18th, the city championship match wasn't as formal as it is today. When he and Van Kampen vied one year in the 36-hole final, Muny was a little too crowded for their liking. "Back in those days it was pretty informal, and one year I was playing Peter in the finals. We got over there and it was crowded as hell, so we played the championship off at Schenectady (Municipal).

"That probably shouldn't be mentioned, but it's true," he said with a smile.

Also, like Hoeffner, Tom Delaney's championship trophy is no more, and all that remains is an 8 x 10 black and white glossy of him holding the impressive statue alongside Mayor Corning. "A gentleman," he said.

He glances over to his wife with a smile. "There's the culprit," he said. "She took my trophy and threw it away."

Tom's wife said, yes, she did toss out the trophy. "I guess I just didn't think he wanted it anymore."

Peter Van Kampen

Not many golfers who once walked the fairways of Albany Muny can boast of playing head-to-head against Arnold Palmer. Peter Van Kampen can.

Van Kampen was another one of those west end boys who got the golf bug caddying at Albany Country Club. It's strange how the proximity to nice private golf courses brings out the golfer in some kids. Beginning at age 13, Van Kampen was toting bags at the old ACC out on Western Avenue, and taking every opportunity to sneak in a few extra rounds with the Delaney brothers and a few other friends.

"During the war, Bob Murray and myself, we used to go over at 5:30 p.m., walk up, start at the second hole and play 18 holes every night. Even when the superintendent caught us a couple of times and said, 'If you guys see anyone on this course and they see you, get out of here.' We said, 'Don't worry about a thing, we'll never cause any problems for you.' And we didn't. We loved that course. It's a crime that Rockefeller took it (for the University at Albany)."

Van Kampen won a pair of city championships during the 1940s but was locked out of the three-peat when he lost to his old friend Tom Delaney in his third final. "He'd deny this, but he was the best putter I ever met. We had some pretty great matches. We were under par by a lot. At that time, we were all playing pretty good golf," he said.

His experience at the old Albany Muny matches that of other golf-hungry young Albanians—long treks across town just to get the chance to play. "We used to walk over there, down Russell Road, with our bags on our shoulders and play 36 holes and then hike all the way home again. We loved the game," he said. "We'd finish 36 holes and then eight guys would go out and play skins. 10 cent skins, 25 cents, whatever."

Van Kampen moved on to Siena College after graduating from Albany High in 1945. There, along with local amateur phenom Billy Shields, he challenged golfers from Ivy League schools, and built up a little more experience on the links of Wolferts Roost, Siena's home course. That college experience was to help in later years when he joined the Loudonville course and won a few club championships.

"That's all ancient history. Now, I just sit back on my accomplishments," he said with a laugh.

Anyway, here's the Arnold Palmer story. In the year before he entered Siena, Van Kampen and Shields finished as the top two in a local qualifier for a national amateur tournament sponsored by the Hearst newspaper chain. The pair, and all the other East Coast qualifiers, were set up on an all-expense paid trip out to Los Angeles. What met them there was the cream of the crop of amateur golf—Billy Maxwell, Bob Rosburg and the young man from Latrobe, Pennsylvania. "Played Arnold Palmer head to head…lost, of course," he said with a smile. "It was a great experience. We played all the good courses, parties in the hotel suite. Billy met Clarke Gable, I think."

Van Kampen links all of his golfing experiences to those early marathon rounds at Albany Muny and the rounds he snuck in at the country club up the street.

"It (Albany Muny) was a rough course back then. Up and down. The sixth hole, you had to hit straight up in the air and had about this much landing area. But it was a municipal golf course. We were just happy that it was there and that we could play it…Golf has been a big part of our lives."

The 1950s

With a newly revised layout to start the decade, the Albany Municipal Golf Course was set for the "golf boom" that swept across the country in the 1950s. People began taking up the game in record numbers, and more significantly, many of those new golfers weren't members of private clubs.

Golf for the working men and women of Albany had been around for two decades but younger kids were now taking up the game with heroes by the name of Palmer and Hogan.

At the muny course, the subtle redesign in 1949 began to have a lasting effect. Many golfers left the mountainous back nine to the younger set, who took to the hilly route like a golfers' boot camp. Holes 10-18 were the realm of teenagers bent on playing 36 holes a day. Later in the day, you might find a pack of amateur hot shots going off 10 for some fairly high stakes skin games.

If Joe Ruszas was the wunderkind of the Muny's early years, Joe Rafferty was the teen star during the 1950s. Rafferty notched three city titles all before hitting his 20s, and he did it against some other young guns and a few players with significantly more experience.

Although the record was subsequently "officially" eclipsed, Larry White insists that he held the amateur scoring record at the course through the 1950s. Nearly five decades later he still remembers the round like it was yesterday, and he's got the newspaper clips to prove a slick 64 over the par 70 layout.

The 1950s also saw the rise of another significant golfing trend—league play, and the Albany Muny course had its share. Named for the popular sporting goods store where it was formed, the Johnny Evers Golf League was to continue at the course for nearly 40 years.

Jack Vogel

"This is what I think about golf. Golf is the greatest game in the world. I started caddying at the old Albany Country Club and I loved every minute of it. Every minute of caddying and playing, and meeting the people. Some of the finest people I ever met were people out there. These were the hoi polloi of the city of Albany, but you'd caddy for them and you'd see the human element. To you, they were just the means to make a dollar.

"What we used to do sometimes when the caddying was slow at the country club. We'd go over to Muny and look for balls, go all over the course and look for them and then we'd stand on the tee and sell them for a quarter, or whatever we could get, and we'd make a little dough that way. This is during the Depression years. We had to do it. I caddied and my three brothers they all caddied. We'd go out and make 90 cents and we'd give 50 cents to my mother to help run the house. In those days if you had a two-dollar day, you were doing pretty well. The best day I ever had was a four-dollar day. I loved it. I loved every minute of it.

"The first time I caddied, I stepped on to the first tee at Albany Country Club and I could feel that nice, soft, moist green under my feet, I said, 'This is for me.' And, really, I kept an interest in other sports, but for me, golf was the only sport that meant anything."

Jack Vogel can tell you a thing or two about the game of golf, a subject he loves to expound on. He'll tell you he wasn't really much of a golfer—had to fight a duck hook when he was younger. Others will tell you he's a fair bit better than he lets on. Golf—watching it, playing it, talking about it—has been a lifelong pastime for Vogel. He and Charlie Rush still get together and play an informal tournament at Mill Road with some old friends each year. He watches and wonders at the feats of a guy he calls "the Tiger," and in the same breath, reminisces about the time he chatted with Byron Nelson at the 1967 US Open at Baltusrol.

"It was the year Nicklaus won it and set the (scoring) record. Afterwards, by a lark, I'm walking by the tent and there they are, (Byron) Nelson and Chris Schenckel. A member's tending bar and he walks over and says, 'You look thirsty.' I say 'yeah,' so he invites me in, and I'm in my glory. Nelson's standing there. He said, 'Did you see Nicklaus? The way he hits the ball, I don't see how anybody can beat him.'"

Like so many others, Vogel's introduction to the game came through caddying, but soon after, he was headed to the local muny, a few cast-off clubs in hand. His first "real" clubs came from a member at Albany Country Club, although they were far from a complete set.

"I was friendly with the guy who ran the pro shop. He was the assistant pro, a guy by the name of Cliff Davis, so when I got finished caddying, I'd go in and help him clean the clubs and put them in their spot. He used to have a machine where he'd buff them and I'd have a rag and wipe 'em off, put them back in the bag. Once in a while members would turn in a set of clubs if they had a new set. Cliff would let me know. This one time a Mrs. Redmond turns in a set of clubs—Robert Tyre Jones clubs, I think Spalding made them—these were some of the top clubs. These are lady irons but the top-line lady irons. I picked up five irons for a buck apiece, 3, 5, 7, 9 and there must have been one other one. Those five irons were used by so many golfers over the years. You don't see this kind of thing these days but kids would go out and we'd all play from the same bag. I never had a full set of clubs until I was in my 30s."

With his friends and fellow ACC caddies, Tom and Warren Delaney, Vogel would make good use of the allotted Monday rounds. Albany Muny filled the remainder of their time on the links.

"When I first joined up to play, you know, with a season pass, it was 10 dollars for the whole year. The whole year! And this was after the war. One year, when we were caddying at Albany Country Club, they restricted our play for some reason. We'd go out on a Monday to Albany Municipal and play all day. We'd start in the morning and we'd play till dark, at least 72 holes or more. There used to be an old guy who was a starter on the old tenth tee. We'd come around and he'd say, 'You kids are going to kill yourselves if you keep playing'"

The marathon rounds only steeled his desire to get better, and with the Delaneys as competition, that was sure to happen.

"This will show you how good those guys were in those days. The last caddy tournament I was in, I was the medallist and I shot a 75, and that's over a tough golf course at the old Albany Country Club. Warren and Tom played in the finals, probably the last caddy tournament they played in. Tom beat his brother 1 up. They both shot a 71, and this was on a par 72 golf course. Tom would have only been 17, 18 years old and Warren just a few years older. Think about it. They didn't have a brand new set of golf clubs, these would have been haphazard sets."

Vogel's best round at Albany Muny—a two-under par 70—came in 1949, just before the course was redesigned.

"It was the first time I ever stood on the 17th tee at even par, and it's a funny feeling. I had a four iron on the old 17th, put it up there within ten feet and made the bird, so now I'm on the 18th at one under. Par five, so it's duck soup for me. I hit a good drive, and I'm hitting a three iron in to the green for my second. I sky the ball. Hit it maybe 100 yards and I'm in front of the green. Hit a nine iron and made the putt. It's not the shots, it's the score."

Lou Weinman

Lou Weinman and his friends were not hustlers, but they certainly enjoyed taking a few bucks off each other now and then. Weinman was just out of high school back in the mid-1950s when he began a regular summer pilgrimage to the Albany Muny course. Although he had frequented the course as a younger kid and played on the Vincentian Institute golf team, it wasn't until age 18 that his real golfing education began.

"I started with my brother and my uncle. They got me out here (to Albany Muny) when I was in the seventh grade. My father was a scratch handicap player out here in the early 1940s. He was in the contracting business. My grandfather, who I was named after, sent me out here to Jerry Dwyer and I spent two summers hanging out, shagging balls. There wasn't a lot of golf going on back then. I played a few nines, but nothing serious."

After high school, Lou went to work for his father in the contracting business, but the golf course was soon filling more and more of his free time.

"When I was 18 and 19 and even 20. Those three years there was when I met (three-time city champ) Frank Hoeffner, and he was really a big influence on me. He taught me a lot of things, just not things about golf, but about the way the world is. He had a lot of good ideas. He read a lot, just a very intelligent guy, and a great birdie shooter. Frank would be having a bad day if he didn't have six birdies, and that's how you make money in the nassaus. Anyway, it was those years, that's when I met all the older fellas out here, good golfers. I got in with these guys who were all about ten years older than I was."

With a fireplug build and a newly discovered Vardon grip, the teen-age Weinman was long off the tee. The regulars called him "Lou with the loop" because of his homemade swing, but he figures at that young age he was a four handicap, even as a self-confessed "lousy wedge player." The older guys must have seen something, because Lou soon became a regular in their weekend nassaus and after work skin games.

"There were a lot of matches going on out here, mostly two-man matches. There were guys who played for a lot of money. $50 nassau, $100 nassau. But the bunch of guys that came from here, we were all used to each other's game. Nobody ever got hurt."

Players would set up matches on the fly, and eventually the contestants traveled to other area clubs to play.

"Eddie Barnett and Walt Gries, both of these guys worked for the railroad, they were engineers. They played for the big money. Tom Hoffman was a good friend of mine. He left here and went to Normanside and then he went to Pinehaven. He and I played in many two-man matches. The most I ever played for was $100 and that was with Gries at Williamstown. He beat me the first time all three ways, plus the skins, and then I came back and shot a 73 at him, and so it was a push. We never played for that much again, but he and Barnett were always playing that $100 nassau. It was a standing thing with them, and they'd play $10 skins, $25 skins once at Ballston Spa.

"The skin games out here were tremendous. There were not many people playing golf, so we'd go out on the back nine in the summer time about 6:00 or 6:30 and we'd have six seven guys in a group. If you were playing $5 skins, you could make some money, better than working. But you know, nobody ever got burned real bad, and if they did they didn't get PO'd about it."

Weinman's hero at the course was Joe Ruszas, probably the hardest working golfer ever to come out of the muny, and its only homegrown State Amateur champ. The Ruszas (Rush) brothers, Charlie and Joe, seemed to be regular fixtures at the muny, even though Charlie was spending much of his time working at golf courses down in Florida. "Joe Rush had a beautiful golf swing. Practiced a lot. Hit a million golf balls. There weren't many fellas that practiced out here. He looked like Ben Hogan, with the cap, and he just had a charisma. I practiced a lot too but it was mostly the short game. The Rush brothers would be around a lot and I'd sit with them and they'd chide me about this and that. Really regular guys. Nice guys. You know before this, I had never really even drank beer or anything. I didn't hang out at the bar. There were guys who would stay and play darts, but I never did."

Like the high stakes nassaus, many of Weinman's playing partners eventually moved on to other clubs. He left the muny in his early 20s and joined Van Schaick Island Country Club, where he became good friends with longtime pro Johnny Gaucas. Eventually, he moved on to McGregor and Wolferts Roost, but a recurring back injury sidelined him at age 31, and he dropped his membership. "I thought I'd never play again, so I quit, broke all the ties to golf, all my people. It was a stupid thing to do."

Lou's back eventually healed and he got back into the game. In 1998, he and a couple of friends from Eagle Crest made it to the national finals of the Oldsmobile Scramble, a team handicap event. He also continued to play the occasional nassau now and then, but not usually for the high stakes of his earlier days.

"Look, when I was 18, 19 years old, I was working for my father. He was paying me $50 a week and I was sometimes making $200 on the golf course. I used to tell him that and it used to burn him up."

Joe Rafferty

By the mid 1950s, a youth movement had arrived at the Muny. Case in point, the youngest city champion ever, Joe Rafferty, who copped the crown at the age of 15 in 1958, and then repeated the feat twice more before leaving his teenage years. Four times a city championship finalist, Rafferty was topped by John Smith in 1960, but came back to beat Smith, his frequent playing companion, in the 1961 final.

Rafferty followed the usual channels into the sport: Albany Country Club caddy, caddy champ, a kid with determination and a lot of time to practice. "Golf just amazed me and I guess I like a challenge," he recalled. "I mean, I was just a hack, but once I got started, I got addicted to it. We would be out there some days 12 or 14 hours straight."

Rafferty was so precocious a talent he won the course's junior tournament the same year he beat good friend Doug Rutnik, then just a 17-year-old himself, for his first city title.

The Saint Joseph's Academy student and his young golfing buddies represented the next generation of golf-crazed kids who made the links their home during the summer months. John and Bob Smith, Andy Kroms, Paul McCarthy, John Sanchirico, Jack Maxstadt, Doug Rutnik, Tom McCabe, Richard and Bob Bates from Bethlehem—just a few names that quickly come to mind for Rafferty. Kid summers in the 1950s. To them, the game of golf meant nothing more than fun, companionship and competition. Maybe that's why so many of them got so good.

"We'd be out there in the pitch dark sometimes," Rafferty remembered. "There was an old oak tree in front of the clubhouse and a bunch of us would go out there after we played and try to hit shots over the tree. We'd see how close we could get to the tree without hitting it. It must have been 25 or 30 feet high. It was just fun stuff like that."

Like the next generation of "muny kids," Rafferty and friends would hook up with the regulars at the course—the few who could provide competition for the young guns. "We'd play quarter skins when these guys, Bill Vogel, Charlie Rush, who would come out after work. A lot of the time we knew we wouldn't get the back nine in so we used to play what we called the back six. 10, 11, and 12, then we'd walk over to the 16th and play in from there," he said. "I thought it was a good course, because it taught you how to hit all kinds of shots. The greens were usually hard as a rock, so you had to hit a high shot into them. I liked the whole course. It was easy but it was a good course for kids to play."

Aside from the three city titles, the highlight of Rafferty's junior career came in 1959 when he finished seventh in a statewide tournament sponsored by the Junior Chamber of Commerce at the Cornell University Golf Course. That year he also competed in the state junior amateur tourney, held at the Garden City Country Club.

Marriage, children and a career with the Albany City Fire Department kept Joe from golf for a decade or so. When he returned to the sport in the early 1970s, he became a member at Brookhaven Country Club, and promptly set that course's amateur scoring record, a 63.

Soon after his retirement from the fire department at age 46, Rafferty and his wife moved to Sebring, Florida. To keep a hand in the game he loved, Joe took a job working at the local muny and discovered he liked it. Five years at Sebring Municipal led to five more years working at the nearby Sun and Lake Country Club. A few years back, the Sebring course offered him a position as assistant course superintendent, and he jumped at it.

With three city championships before the age of 19, Rafferty said he thought briefly about turning to the professional ranks as a young man. "Back in those days there wasn't any qualifying school. You just had to find someone to back you for $25,000. I thought about it for awhile, but I don't have any regrets."

Larry White

Like most good golfers, Larry White often remembers the shots he missed more the ones he made. White shot an amateur course record 64 in 1955, but when asked to describe the round, the first thing he said was, "missed a six-foot birdie on the first, missed a six-foot birdie on the seventh."

Forty-five years after the deed that put him in the record book, it's as if those two shots were still haunting him, keeping him from the 62 he casually let slip through his hands. But White was anything but casual about golf, and especially putting.

Every weekday the sun shone on Albany Municipal Golf Course, White would leave his job as a draftsman at Albany Design Company and hurry over to beat the league players who clogged up the course beginning at 5 p.m.

At age 25, he had been playing golf for 10 years, first at Pine Brook Country Club in Gloversville, but since his job took him to Albany, more recently at the muny course. White also traveled the amateur tournament circuit, which brought him to the area's numerous private clubs.

His game was suited to courses like Albany, short and straightforward; a course where a drive down the middle and a good short game can overcome almost anything. White admits that he never hit the ball a very long way, but the putter was his ace in the hole, the weapon that helped him tame the Muny 18. Even some 40 years later, White has the look of a "grinder," a guy who takes it personally when birdie putts don't fall. "I had nine putts on nine holes on many courses," said White with unassuming pride. "When the putter was going, I could shoot low."

The hot putter and his steady play came together on a mid-summer Thursday in 1955. It was just like any other weekday he left work on North Broadway and hurried over to Muny. White hooked up with Dick Van Kampen and the two went off for a quick 18, a jump ahead of the leagues.

After the missed birdie opportunity on the first, White found his pace. Four birdies came on the front nine—one of them on the course's trickiest hole, the par-three eighth. His only bogey was on the par-three sixth. All in all, a very respectable front nine—out in three-under 32.

"The back nine started out bogey, bogey, at 10 and 11, and I thought to myself, 'I just ruined a good round.'"

But White wasn't giving up. As it had the past, his putter came through and he blistered holes 12 through 16 with five straight birdies. Another six-foot birdie putt on the 17th stopped on the lip and, on 18, a two-putt from 30 feet sealed an easy par. The Gloversville native had carded another 32, for a total 64, two strokes better than the previous amateur mark set in 1953 by Ronnie Terpak, a golfer from Endicott.

Albany Muny was a convenient and cheap place to satisfy White's daily need for the links, but he didn't think much of the course. In fact, he hated it.

"Worse course I ever played," he said. "The course they have out there now is a good course for a kid to grow up on, but the old course was not the same." Even so, he and the muny are tied together in the record books.

White's record round was no fluke. Throughout the 1950s, he made it to the state amateur tournament four times, but his stellar efforts in local qualifying did him little good at the state level.

"One-round White," he said with a smile and a shrug. "I did face a lot of tough guys in the first round. I'd get on these long courses, and have to hit long irons into greens..." Another shrug, another tiny smile.

White made it to the match play State Am in 1952, 1953, 1955 and 1959, and he did compete in a lot of local tournaments. His best story comes from the 1956 Mayor's Cup final at Muny.

"Jack Reilly beat me in the final," he recalled. "Thirty-six hole match play in, it must have been 90 degree heat. It may have been hotter, but anyway, it was hot. We finished and I decided to drive up to Warner's Lake to go for a swim and cool down. I jump in and my knees just locked. Hot weather, cool water. I had to paddle in," he said. Albany's hills had claimed another victim.

White's record 64 was matched three years later by a retired Albany Policeman Jim "Red" Williams. "It was the easiest round of golf I ever played," Williams, then 50, told a local sportswriter. The *Times Union* reported, however that Williams "had broken the amateur course record," which they incorrectly claimed, was "shared jointly by a pair of out-of-towners."

In 1963, Albany's two daily newspapers reported two more low rounds at the "old course," but again the lack of editorial oversight leaves these records in some doubt. Andy Kroms, according to a two-paragraph blurb in the *TU*, tied the record set by White and Williams, with a 64. But the *Knickerbocker News* reported that Kroms had "shattered the amateur course record at Albany Municipal when he carded a seven-under-par 70," and said, "he went out in 32 and came home in 31 on the par 35-35-70 course." Obviously, seven-under is not 70, and since the *TU* reported that Kroms tied the record not beat it, as the Knick reported, White feels comfortable knowing his mark was safe—or at least just tied.

Other Muny golfers remember Kroms, a two-time city champion, as an effective but unorthodox golfer. "He was one of those fellows who looked like he was swinging in a phone booth, but he was an excellent player," said one.

Amazingly, just a month after Kroms' round, the record was tied again by Harold Menchel, who carded another six-under round. "Oddly enough," the *TU* wrote," Menchel was playing with Kroms…when he carded his 64."

Like the golfer who marks his scorecard after every hole, Larry White has all of these newspaper clips handy, duly noted in his draftsman's straight lettering where the papers made their editorial mistakes. "I just wanted to make sure you got this right," he said.

Bob Kisselback

If not for a few rainy Sundays, one of the longest tenured golf leagues at Albany Muny may have played their matches at Western Turnpike instead of out on New Scotland Avenue. When the charter members of the Johnny Evers Golf League gathered in the back room of the Johnny Evers Sporting Goods store on State Street, they initially decided on the Guilderland course to play their matches, remembers Bob Kisselback, but "it rained, rained, rained for the first couple of Sundays we were out there, so we went over to Muny and we ended up staying."

By the time the Johnny Evers group came along in the late 1950s, golf leagues had already been fairly well established at the course, mostly by area fraternal organizations like the Knights of Columbus and the Elks, as well as the local Roman Catholic parish, St. Catherine's. What set the Evers crew apart were its members. To a man, they were ex-jocks, high school heroes of the basketball court and baseball diamond, many of whom had gone on to become referees and other officials for interscholastic sports.

"The whole thing started in the back room of the Johnny Evers Sporting Goods store, which was a hangout for jocks," Kisselback said. "Pete Horan, who was a prominent ref in the area, ran the place with Joe Evers. Pete was one of the charter members. Joe didn't play much golf, he was the nephew of Johnny Evers. We got the Friday night slot at Albany Muny and we had one standing rule—you showed up no matter what. It could be pouring rain and if you didn't show up you had to forfeit your match. We were out to have a good time and that was it. We'd shoot darts, play some cards if the weather wasn't good."

Charter members included Horan and Kisselback, Ray McLeer, "Bull" McMullin, Rod O'Connor, Hugo Pellechi, Tom Burke, Bill Bernardo, George Bruda, Ed Sowek, Frank Staucet, "Bus" Riley, Dick Bogdan, Bill Huff, Leo Mullin, Larry O'Neill, Bob Powell and a few others that Kisselback said his poor memory doesn't allow him to recall. "A lot of these guys are gone now," he said with regret.

The Evers League group was a tight bunch, Ed Sowek recalled. "They were a great bunch of guys. The kind that if you called them at three in the morning, you wouldn't get a question, you'd get 'How can I help you?'"

Each year, league members would have a two-man championship tourney, and, in a bid to appease wives who sat home alone on Friday nights, a dinner to which spouses were invited. With that taken care of, the guys would head up for a weekend of fun in the Adirondacks at a place in Indian Lake. Kisselback didn't provide many details on what activities took place up there. Perhaps that's a story in itself.

The league's membership came and went over the next 30 years, but they never expanded beyond a few dozen players and they rarely strayed from the core of ex-jocks looking for a competitive golf game. "I'm biased, of course, but I'd say we were the premier league in the area," said Kisselback, who played until the 1980s.

The league lasted through the transition to the new course and was going along until the late 1990s, when the city decided to open up afternoon play for non-league golfers. Squeezed out of their traditional Friday evening slot, the Johnny Evers League ironically ended up back where they originally started. Today, they play league matches at the Western Turnpike Golf Course, where it allegedly rains no more than it does in Albany.

The 1960s

The 1960s was a transitional time for the old Muny. With the decade half over, the passing of longtime pro Jerry Dwyer signaled a serious decline in activity. No city championships would be held at the course for the next 25 years and a string of amateur "pros" would man the clubhouse until the 1990s. Those first few years of the 1960s, however, saw the increasing growth of youth golf at the course, all under the tutelage of one man who seemed to disappear as mysteriously as he appeared—Clem McMahon. What was once a rag tag group of young golfers would become a dominating force in local golfing circles and place the young muny hotshots consistently ahead of their counterparts from the area's private clubs.

The Junior Champs

Hollywood would love this script. Take a handful of young city kids hungry for golf, rising every summer morning to bike over to the local muny. Side bets for quarters, milk shakes and hamburgers at the turn, joking, and just loving the idea that a $10 season pass provides 36 holes a day, sometimes more. Golf all day, every day. The course is a goat path, deserted on the back nine, dry as a dust bowl in summer. They don't care. They thrive on the awkward angles, dirt tees; and eventually they get pretty good—12-year-olds breaking 90 without breaking a sweat.

Enter a mystery figure. He just shows up one summer with a city job at the course—an older guy with brushed back hair. The kids learn he's a World War II vet, shot up good in the Philippines. Lost a leg, part of his shoulder. The old vet takes an interest in the tireless young golfers, and he sees an opportunity, a chance for them to take their competition on the road against the kids from the private clubs.

They load up in the back of the old man's station wagon twice a week and hit the road. Edison Club, Normanside, Troy Country Club—milk shakes and hamburgers whether they win or lose. The thing is, they hardly ever lose. The country club boys aren't much of a match for the muny kids, and the defeats are embarrassing—14 ½ to ½, 15 to 0. The only fierce competition comes from the area's other muny teams, Schenectady and Troy's Frear Park.

The story may sound a little "Tin Cup" but it's true. During the early 1960s, Albany Municipal built a junior golf program that was the envy of the area, and, along the way, it became the starting point for some of the area's best amateur golfers.

"If you look at how well we did against the country club teams, it was a factor of us having free and open access to golf," said Charlie Murphy, a muny kid who went on to become a three-time State Amateur runner-up, and compete in two USGA national championships, as well as the British Amateur. "Those (private club) kids had the pool to go to, they had tennis, but most importantly they had restricted access to golf. Many of them couldn't play until the afternoon. We had access to golf 14 hours a day. They subtly shot us over to the back nine, but I can remember playing the back nine five times in one day, more than a few times. We could literally play golf all day."

Murphy and Mike Daniels, who would later set the course record at the tender age of 16, formed the core of a generation of "muny kids," the kind that would hop on their bikes and take the ride down New Scotland every day the sun was shining.

"We basically started golf and gave up all other sports. We had a locker, and came here, every day, every day, every day," Murphy said, repeating the phrase for emphasis. "It would be my mother dropping me off or us taking the bikes, and we would get here at 7:30 a.m. and we would go home at 9 p.m. Often we would go to Tommy Connery's house on Ferndale and continue putting through his house when we finished. The golf was from sunrise to sunset and, for me, that was from age 11 through college."

Murphy and Daniels would be tied together by their golfing exploits throughout their younger years and they still remain competitive amateurs. Their friendship began on the baseball diamond of National Little League, and with their neighboring homes on West Lawrence and South Pine.

"We were Little League pals and we decided to take up golf," said Daniels. "I think our parents both got us our first set of clubs when we were 12, after that it was every day. Our folks would come out and pick us up at dark. They loved it because they always knew where we were."

Both players took to the game, the atmosphere, and especially the competition. They'd watch the older golfers, and imitate swings. Once in a while, "the old pro," Jerry Dwyer would notice something and give advice, but it was the grinding rounds and the grueling hills that honed their games; loop after loop along the back nine. At age 13, Daniels won the city's junior tournament (ages 11-13 division) with a 78. "I knew we were getting good when the winner of the older division shot an 80," he remembered.

There was a slightly older contingent of players who served as golfing role models for the youngsters who would dominate the junior inter-league series in the early 1960s.

"There was our group, (Mike) Bloom, (Harold) Menchel, Howard Schulman, (Steve) Hutchins, (Tom) Connery, Bob Smith, Richie Maxstadt, we were all about the same age," said Murphy. "Then there was a group that was, in our eyes, slightly older. Joe Rafferty, John Smith, Andy Kroms, those are the three I remember. They hit the ball a long way. We were young and impressionable enough to go out and sit on the bench and watch them hit off the tenth tee. Wound balls and persimmon woods, they all hit the ball and it started out really low and it rose. A trajectory you just don't see today."

Both Daniels and Murphy don't mention much about lessons during those early years. It was mostly just watch, absorb and tromp around the course with Hoganesque determination. But for all their endless summer days of golfing, tinkering with swings, chipping balls over the maple tree in front of the clubhouse, putting on the carpet of Tommy Connery's house, it was just a bunch of kids having fun.

Then Clem showed up.

Looking back, and remembering from a child's perspective, Clem McMahon truly was a mystery figure. Sometime in the spring of either 1961 or 1962, he arrived at the course, several years removed from the Veterans Administration hospitals where he learned to walk with a prosthetic leg, and learned to cope with the other serious injuries suffered in combat on the Philippine island of Mindanao. No one remembers where he came from and no one clearly remembers much about his past, aside from his veteran status and his relationship with local VFW Post 1019, the Oppenheim Post. It was McMahon's standing at the post that helped the group of young guns get the chance to travel to some of the area's most exclusive courses.

"He got the veterans to sponsor us as a junior team from Albany Municipal to play against various clubs in the area. The veterans actually paid for golf balls, shirts, hats. We had a uniform," Daniels remembered. "We started this junior interclub. I think it eventually got to be six teams in each division, two divisions. We played Edison, Albany Country Club, Colonie, Shaker Ridge, Normanside, and so each week we got on the private courses in the area. Clem used to drive us around in his 1963 green and white Pontiac station wagon, and we would all climb into the station wagon. You'd never see this today—six kids with golf bags in a station wagon—but this was back in the 60s and our parents let us do it. He drove us all over to play these matches, and it was phenomenal for us."

"All of the sudden out of nowhere, Clem McMahon showed up," said Murphy. "You asked me what was enchanting about the game, and part of it was this mystery guy who shows up in an old Pontiac station wagon, and he forms a junior team. He consolidated what was ragamuffin stuff into playing for the course and playing for the VFW, and that gave structure to everything. We came along, Clem came along and it just came together. He took the kids under his wing."

Murphy remembers with a cynical smile the uniforms that were provided by the veterans. "They were made out of Banlon. Remember Banlon? It was hotter than the devil and they had this enormous VFW patch on the chest. That patch would throw off our backswing. Mike was the only it didn't bother because he was a leftie."

With more than a dozen kids vying to play on his squad, McMahon kept the competitive fires burning by putting up a small stake to play for, among the Muny regulars.

"He used to dip into his pocket—50 cents or a dollar—to let us play on a regular basis during the course of a week. We'd go out and play 18 holes and whoever won got a free lunch that day," Daniels said. "This guy did so much for us. He and Jerry Dwyer."

In 1962, the Muny group topped the teen players from Nick Stoner in Caroga Lake to take the Northeastern New York PGA Junior Golf League crown. Daniels said the group from Albany might have won the inter-league title, or at least the divisional title, four out of the six years he competed for the squad.

The Schenectady Muny team, which through the early 1960s featured Jimmy and Bob Duval (better known as David's father), as well as future local pro Ron Philo (father of the LPGA's Laura Diaz), was always the squad to beat, Murphy remembered. He also recalls being envious of the layout the Electric City boys represented. "We were jealous of that Schenectady Muny course. We thought it was great," he said.

As both a player and a course employee for nearly his entire young life, Murphy has a bagful of stories from the Muny. His playing days turned a corner in 1964, when he was medallist in the sectional tournament for the USGA Junior Amateur tournament. Murphy traveled to Eugene, Oregon, to play in the event, and eventually got to the round of 32 before bowing out. A youngster named Johnny Miller won the tournament. A week after his qualifying, he also won the local qualifier for the New York State Junior Amateur.

While Murphy was finding his fortune off the muny course in 1964, Daniels was making history back home. On July 25, the youngster toured the New Scotland Avenue layout in 61, nine shots under par, and easily a new course record.

Daniels played the back nine first, with Tom Connery, and shot a sizzling 32. His partner on the front was another longtime muny golfer, Mel Levy, and it was here he caught fire. Birdies on 4, 6, 7 and 8 and an eagle on the ninth hole sealed a six-under for the front side and the record round of 61.

"Author of three 31s on the front nine and two 66s for the 18 earlier in the year, Daniels used only 24 putts en route to this 9-under-par achievement," the *Times Union* reported.

Slowly, the muny kids outgrew the inter-club team, and a few moved on to private clubs. Clem lasted until the later 1960s but then moved along as mysteriously as he arrived. The death of Jerry Dwyer in 1965 spelled the downfall of a lot of activity at the course, and by the latter part of the decade the junior program was no more. Even in his later years, Dwyer's energy and enthusiasm for the course drew a myriad of events—cancer benefits, other charity events, junior/senior matches. Much of it slowly dwindled away with his passing.

Murphy and Daniels kept at it, however, with the former taking a series of jobs at the course through his teenage years.

"Started when I was 16 in 1963 and I was a cashier in the old clubhouse," he said. "I would take the dollar during the week and a dollar and a quarter on the weekends, and crank out a Moore business form, which was the receipt and also the paper score card. I'm pretty sure that I was the only one that never took one of those dollars. The old timers would pay their dollars or they'd have a season pass, and they didn't want a score card, so if you were good at it you could keep the dollar, but I never did."

Murphy moved from his clubhouse job to a position as night watch-men and eventually he joined the course's grounds crew. "Roy Salis-bury was the superintendent and he had a night job at a supermarket over off Orange Street, and I always thought that was curious," he remembered. "I primarily cut greens. There were old timers who they would entrust mowing the fairways. If you look at the hills, it was haz-ardous to your health. We had the old Arnold Palmer Toro tractor and the Toro greens mower. The younger guys were given the greens or aprons to mow."

Although he had by then secured a membership at the new Pine-haven golf course, Murphy, who played high school golf at Vincentian Institute and college golf for Siena, continued working at the city course through his college years; he was a night bartender for Jack McCaffrey. "My father, who was a muny golfer and had never been the member of a private club, got a membership at Pinehaven. One of the reasons he did it was so that I could get into certain tournaments that were restricted to golfers affiliated with a private club."

Working in the clubhouse taproom opened Murphy's eyes a bit. He'd seen the denizens of the darkened bar come and go at all hours of the day during his younger years. Now working the bar himself, he got to know the colorful crew of barstool sages.

Murphy moved from Pinehaven to McGregor to Albany Country Club and eventually settled at Wolferts Roost, where he's stayed since. But his time at the Muny, from Clem McMahon and Jerry Dwyer through McCaffrey and new pro Bob Moore, was the genesis for all his golfing success, and it has an unmovable place in his memory.

Daniels also continued to play at the Muny through his teenage years. He played high school golf for Vincentian Institute and Albany High. At Hudson Valley Community College, he was sectional medal-list and twice qualified for the National Junior College Athletic Associ-ation tournament. Transferring to Siena, he also played for its golf team.

Seven years after joining Normanside Country Club in 1970, he set a course record 62 there and currently he plays out of Shaker Ridge. Daniels continues to have a stellar career as an amateur golfer and even has made the sport of golf his business. He owns "Gifts Fore the Golfer," a national operation that sells golf antiques, memorabilia, photography and other collectibles.

Of the rest of the 1960s "golden boys,"—Menchel, Maxstadt, Smith, Bloom and the rest—several still live and work in the area, and others return on an annual basis to visit family, friends and play in the occasional invitational tournament.

No one I've talked to knows what happened to Clem McMahon. He was in his late 50s during the boys' heyday, so perhaps he moved on to another municipal course to work his magic. What's certain is the effect he had on the group at Albany Muny, especially Daniels. "This guy did so much for us," he said. "He just took us under his wing and created this whole junior golf thing. If he hadn't come along, it probably wouldn't have happened at all."

The 1970s–1980s

Rundown, neglected, forgotten and abused. Well, perhaps it wasn't that bad, but if there was a "dark ages" for the Albany Municipal Golf Course, it probably took place during the last two decades of its original incarnation—the 1970s and 1980s. Any golf course operator will tell you that it takes a constant influx of money to maintain a certain level of playability, and the muny just wasn't getting that injection. While the course was still a nominal moneymaker for the city, the Corning administration had let benign neglect, rampant patronage and a goat track reputation take over. What other course in the area could say that it didn't allow motorized golf carts because of the insurance liability?

But there were tees (which had a reputation all their own) fairways (unwatered) and greens with a hole that measured the standard 4 ¼ inches in circumference. It might not have been Pebble Beach or Merion, but for the faithful, it was their course. Despite and maybe because of its condition, people still loved the Muny with a passion. And, it should be mentioned, the place was still an incredible bargain. In 1970, a season membership was only $20, and a single round during the week cost a buck. That's right. One dollar. In 1974, the membership costs jumped to $30 and the 18-hole rate was pushed up to two dollars. Still probably the cheapest 18 holes in the area.

Leagues continued to flourish at the course and even in the mid-1970s, the course was reporting about 45,000 rounds a season. But by the early 1980s, the course was clearly showing its age. Bunkers around some of the greens contained ever diminishing amounts of sand and the condition of the tees were so bad that some golfers had taken to creating their own teeing grounds.

Golf junkies, both of the old and young variety, still called Muny home, with the predictable delineation between those who played the front (older guys) and those who favored the back nine (young guys with strong legs). Many of those younger players went on to become top-flight amateurs and two grew up to become Class A PGA professionals in the area—Jim Jeffers and Peter Gerard.

Jim Jeffers

A round of golf can be a lot more enjoyable with the right partners. Jim Jeffers, the head professional at Eagle Crest Golf Club in Clifton Park, learned that lesson early. As a teenaged "muny kid" with a reputation as a long hitter, Jeffers was another one of those 6 a.m. to 9 p.m. grinders. Not that he minded. "For a few years, it was my whole life in the summer," he said. "We would get there as early as possible, play all day and leave around 9 p.m."

What made Jeffers a bit different from his youthful golf compadres, however, was his choice of partners. "I befriended a lot of the older guys. The stories you heard from some of these guys who had played there for years, well, they were pretty incredible. I was 17 in 1978 and I got to know Ted Rau, who was the self-proclaimed pro at the time. Ted had the only golf cart on the course and it was always getting stuck, but, I'll tell you, he taught me how to play."

Jeffers, whose family hailed from the Whitehall Road area, soaked in as much history as possible on those rounds with his older friends. Along the way, a little golfing knowledge got passed down as well. "I remember Charlie Rush, Joe Rush, Chet Roman, Charlie Praeger, Tom Delaney, these guys were all pretty decent golfers. You'd talk to the older guys and listen to their stories," Jeffers said.

Jeffers said he thought about writing down some of his golfing companions' stories. He never got around to that, but the stories are ready for telling. Here's a small sampling, told second hand:

The classic Albany Muny story that Jeffers passes down is one involving Al Capone. Apparently the Chicago mob boss was passing through our fair capital some time in the 1930s and looking for a quick round on the links. Capone allegedly coughed up enough cash to have the front nine closed to all but himself and his entourage, free to roam the hills of Albany Muny without the threat of prying eyes.

The Eagle Crest pro also remembers an old-timer, a man he recalls only by the name Izzy, who told Jeffers he was the warm up catcher for Babe Ruth during his years with the Red Sox. "This guy used to play (golf) in regular baseball cleats, and he wasn't too bad. He said he used to catch for Babe Ruth with the Red Sox, and when the Babe was traded to the Yankees, he went along with him as his warm up catcher. It was part of the contract."

Tales of Albany Municipal's infamous hills are readily accessible from Jeffers' memory. A quick loop around the back nine one afternoon turned into a segment out of "Emergency."

"Joel Skolnik and I were walking up to the 15th and there's this guy who was hunched over. We thought he was tying his shoes but the closer we get, we see that his face is blue! Joel and I took turns carry him on our backs to the clubhouse."

If the creek was low, Jeffers and his younger playing partners were not above enjoying the plusher fairways of Normanside Country Club, located just a few hops over the Normanskill. More than a few times they were sent rushing back across the creek followed by iron shots launched by Normanside pro Ralph Montoya. "I think they were five irons he was hitting at us," he recalls, with a laugh.

He remembers fist fights on the second green, women getting beaned by errant drives on the sixth ("she went down fast...hit her right between the eyes") and a golfer by the name of "Red" Howard, who invariably wore red clothes ("red hat, red shirt, red socks, everything"). But the comic relief that was an undercurrent at Albany Muny was secondary to the game itself. Jeffers was a grinder, and he knew the days of trudging the back nine were paying off. Watching him hit from an adjacent fairway one day, three-time city champ Tom Delaney told him, "You're going to be a player, kid."

Teenagers take those comments to heart, and within a few years Jeffers was considering a life as a teaching pro. At age 20 or 21, he was offered a position at Pinehaven in Guilderland, where he worked for five years. Then it was on to the Edison Club and, eventually, his post at Eagle Crest.

Despite his spot at one of the area's nicer public layouts, Jeffers still has soft spot for the billygoat hills of Albany Muny.

"I think it's nice that the course has been rebuilt, but to be honest, I'd like to have the old course back. There was something about it. You got used to every lie you could imagine. I'm proud to say that I grew up playing that course. It was distinctive. You could play anywhere in the country and not face some of the lies you'd see there every day."

Peter Gerard

Although the highly successful junior interclub program was a mere memory by the early 1970s, a new crop of young golfers was making Albany Muny their summer hangout of choice. A few years before Jim Jeffers joined up with his older cronies, a new generation of Whitehall Road kids were trekking devotedly around the Muny back nine. Among them was Peter Gerard, whose family lived on Maxwell Street. Gerard is currently the head professional at Orchard Creek Golf course and, like Jeffers, is considered one of the area's best teaching pros. He's a three-time Northeastern New York PGA Player of the Year and two-time NENYPGA Teacher of the Year. He's also twice been nominated for *Golf* magazine's Top 100 Teachers list.

Peter figures he was about 8 or 9 years old when he began playing along with his brothers Michael and Bill. "At one time, there were a ton of kids out there. They weren't all from our neighborhood. We'd walk out there from Whitehall Road and some of us had lockers. We got on the front nine every now and then, but we mostly stuck to the back nine," he recalled.

It was the same story as the previous generations of muny kids. "Twenty-seven or 36 holes a day sometimes. That wasn't unusual," he said. "It was a daily diet of uneven lies, and I think that does something good for your golf game. It forces you to learn a variety of different shots."

Gerard tells an oft-told tale—young kid becomes fascinated with the game and practices like crazy to get better. "We'd go out there and play two balls a hole. The back nine was ours and we'd practice out there. I'd say 'I'm going to hit high hooks' and I'd try to hit a bunch of them and my brother or whoever I was with would hit them back. Eventually, with that kind of practice, a lot of these guys were able to make the ball do what they wanted to do. That's what was captivating about the game. You could go out and practice as much as you wanted and you could do it by yourself, if no one was around."

Gerard mentions a few names when asked who else was playing out there during the early 1970s. John Deitz, Kevin Cassidy, Jim Waldbillig, Jim Betzwieser and John Gadani come to mind, but he said there certainly were more who were considered regulars. "We used to sit and watch guys like Tom Venter and Charlie Murphy. They were several years older, but Venter, he could hit like you'd see Daley or Tiger Woods hit it today. I was just a little kid, and I remember not believing that someone could hit a golf ball like that."

With his buddies, many from the Saint Catherine's and Saint Teresa's parishes near the course, Gerard captained one of the powerhouse high school golf teams in Section II history, from Vincentian Institute/ Bishop Maginn. Gerard said the team from the late 1970s would sometimes shoot a gross average 33 or 34 for nine holes. "And the majority of the guys on that team were self-taught," he said.

After high school, Gerard walked away from the game for about five years. He was working in the human services field at Albany's Cerebral Palsy Center when he took up the game again. Cassidy, a fellow muny kid, had taken an assistant pro job at Normanside and helped Gerard get a similar position at Evergreen. From there, he moved on to Wolferts Roost, and then opened his own golf school at Mill Road Acres. In 2000, he found his current position—head pro at Orchard Creek. Two years later, the course was hailed by *Golf Digest* as the "Best New Bargain" in the country and Gerard has been busy ever since.

Gerard's greatest memory from the Muny is a round of 59, which he shot while still in high school. Although he doesn't recall many specifics he knows he carded a few eagles. "You have to remember that this was before watered fairways. The conditions were hard a lot of the time, so you would get a lot of run on the ball," he said.

With the Muny's shorter par fours and fives, Gerard was probably able to set up quite a few birdie and eagle opportunities.

"The place forced you to make shots," he said. "It was a real education."

Albany Municipal—18 Holes
Three Different Ways

The Original 18—The original par 72 Albany Municipal Golf course was constructed over a period of about seven months in 1931, and despite its unusual layout, it quickly became a recreational hot spot for the working men and women of the Capital District. At the time of its construction, Albany Muny was the only publicly owned 18-hole golf course in the area (Frear Park was then only 9 holes). On average, during its early years, about 30,000 golfers paid the small fee each year to satisfy their lust for the links. The course fulfilled Mayor John Boyd Thacher's goal of "paying for itself."

Because the course was re-routed prior to the 1950 season, it is difficult to find people who recalled the original 18. Most Albany duffers would, however, recognize all but two of the holes. The layout was re-configured in an effort to "flatten the course," but the holes were essentially the same. The original design had the front nine snaking around a perimeter of holes that comprised the original back nine. The four hilliest holes (13 through 16 on the post-1949 course) were split between the front and back nines, saving the golfer from back-to-back climbs.

"What they did was put most of the hilly holes on the back nine," said Ed Huba, who played the course for half a century. "It just made people want to play the front nine and leave the climbing to the kids."

Here is a rundown of the original 18, with some commentary. More detailed information is contained in the following section, which discusses the course following the 1949 redesign.

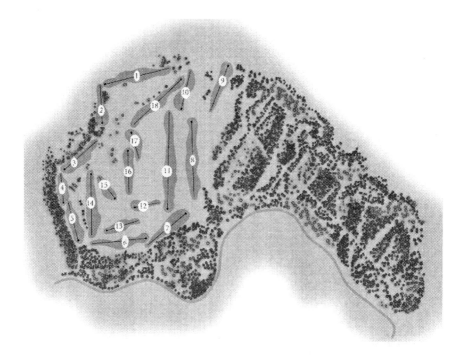

First hole—Par 5—455 yards—Stand on the current first tee and turn about 40 degrees to your right. Beyond two mounds, on the right side of the stand of trees, stood the first green of the original course. If course architect John Melville was preparing you for the strenuous task ahead, he couldn't have chosen a better route. Looking at the landscape now, it seems ridiculous that this should have been the opening hole. Your drive, if more than 200 yards, would land at the bottom of a small gully, leaving you a semi-blind shot to the green, another hill away. This hole was rightly one of the first considered for elimination when the course was redesigned in 1949.

Second hole—Par 4—341 yards—A hole that faced total elimination in the 1949 redesign, and remnants of it are now hard to find. The tee was located past the original first green, up near the city's community garden off Hartman Road. Although a group of trees now blocks the way, the hole itself cut down along the property line and the green was located in front of the second tee. "There used to be a fella by the name of Fred Capasella who was a musician, and he sat up about 40 or 50 yards in front of the second green and he would blow a bugle to tell you to come on," remembers Huba.

Third hole—Par 4—278 yards—With the elimination of the old second hole, this short par 4 became the second hole of the 1950 layout.

Fourth hole—Par 3—135 yards—Course architect Melville finally found a flat piece of ground to work on and he laid out a short par 3. This became the third hole following the 1949 redesign.

Fifth hole—Par 4—298 yards—The original fifth hole became the Muny's fourth hole after 1949; another short, straight track along the edge of the trees. As with the previous hole, the trouble was either long or right.

Sixth hole—Par 4—348 yards—The original sixth became the dreaded 15, part of the string of torturous holes that made the muny back nine a legend. A wooden bridge was constructed here by public works crews to help negotiate the deep valley. On the original layout, this was the start of the loop that wrapped the front nine around the back nine.

Seventh hole—Par 4—289 yards—The seventh hole continued across the gullies and would become the 16th hole after the redesign. Another hole where a bridge was deemed necessary to negotiate the climb. It was added as part of a WPA project in the late 1930s.

Eighth hole—Par 5—487 yards—The second par 5 on the original front nine, this became the 17th hole after the redesign. Until it was taken down in the 1950s, golfers could catch a glimpse of the O'Neil dairy farm, located on the site of the current seventh green.

Ninth hole—Par 4—388 yards—Completing the loop around the inner holes, the ninth hole became the 18th after the redesign.

Tenth hole—Par 4—361 yards—The only hole on the original back nine which remained virtually unchanged after 1950, the tenth followed the left side of the current driving range. A large three-pocket bunker guarded the left side of the green. A picture of this green is shown in the 1932 Mayor's Report to the Common Council. The stand of trees that now backs up the left side of the Capital Hills driving range is non-existent, just a few spindly pines.

Eleventh hole—Par 5—505 yards—This par 5 was reduced to a par four in the 1949 overhaul and became the 12th hole. The original tee was back further and golfers had to carry a small ravine before reaching the wide-open fairway.

Twelfth hole—Par 3—125 yards—The 12th became the 13th following the redesign. Once again, course architect John Melville found himself at the end of a valley with no place to go except across. The first of the gully holes on the original back nine and another where a bridge helped golfers in the valley crossing.

Thirteenth hole—Par 4—243 yards—Course architect Melville again ventured across the gullies on this short par 4, which became the 14th hole after the redesign. Another gully, another bridge.

Fourteenth hole—Par 4—415 yards—Probably the most challenging hole in the original design, simply because of its length and the fact that sliced shots to the green fell down the flanking hillside. This became the fifth hole after the redesign but was listed as 382 yards, nearly 30 yards shorter than its original length.

Fifteenth hole—Par 3—166 yards—This par 3 became the sixth on the 1950 scorecard, but otherwise was basically unchanged. Pictures of the 15th and 14th holes taken in the early 1930s reveal how few trees were on this part of the course, just wide open rolling hills and a few stairs to help start the climb down to the green set on a plateau.

Sixteenth hole—Par 4—282 yards—A short trip up the hill from the 15th green and you ended up back in the middle valley. This short par 4 to an elevated green became the seventh hole.

Seventeenth hole—Par 3—180 yards—The third par 3 in seven holes, the 17th hole featured a difficult uphill carry to a two-tiered green. It was probably much more difficult with hickory shafted clubs and wound balls back in the 1930s. This became the eighth hole.

Eighteenth hole—Par 5—507 yards—The short par 5 home hole became the ninth after the redesign. Although there was little trouble off the tee and on the approach, the 18th was listed as the number one handicap hole. Pictures of the hole from the 1930s show two large bunkers on the left.

The 1950 Scorecard—Take a look at the distances on this score-card and you'd think Albany Municipal was a real pushover. Well, if you knew the course and had a fairly decent cardiovascular system, it might be. For above average golfers, most of the par fours left a rela-tively short approach and the par fives could easily be reached in two. The problems came for the average hacker and weekend duffer, who would often find their balls sliced into dense thicket or in lies so unusual that a proper stance became impossible.

"That's one of the things about Albany Muny," said Mike Daniels, a top local amateur who spent many a youthful summer day at the course during the late 1950s and early 1960s. "You learned how to hit a real variety of shots because you hardly ever had a flat lie. Guys who played on flat courses had a lot of trouble playing there."

A quick note for anyone who wants to explore the old course for nostalgia or exercise. Most of the old, yellow-painted tee markers are still in place, where they don't interfere with the new course layout. If you're feeling adventurous, the guide rails on holes 6, 13, 14, 16 and 17 are still somewhat intact. If you remember the old course, it's pretty easy to follow until you get to the back nine. Proceed with caution on any hole from 13 through 16. It's amazing how quickly nature can overtake a piece of land after just 10 years. And with the added conges-tion of briar patches, saplings and fallen trees, those hills are still a tough climb.

Here is a rundown of the Albany Municipal course following the 1949 redesign.

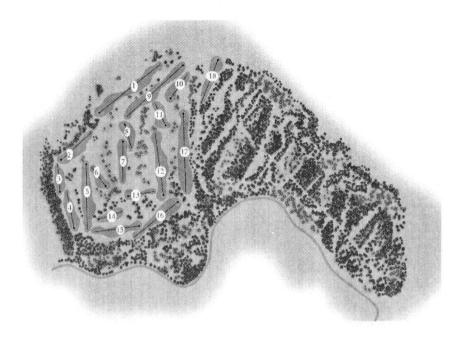

First hole—Par 5—513 yards—After the original first hole was abandoned in the fall of 1949, a few trees were removed from the current first fairway. The first hole became a nice opening par 5, with a small green that left little room for inaccuracy.

Second hole—Par 4—288 yards—Leave the first green to the left and you'll notice the remains of a well-worn footpath through the woods. This path took golfers to the tee of the second hole, a short par 4 with an open plateau landing area.

An old Muny golfer told the story of a duffer who once swung so hard on the second tee that he fell down the hill behind the tee box. If you look down the ravine behind the old second tee now, you'll find a pair of old concrete benches, discarded to make way for the newer hole. According to former muny kid and current Eagle Crest head pro Jim Jeffers, the second hole saw its share of fistfights. With long hitters able to reach a relatively blind green on their drive, there were often confrontations. In winter, the outline of the small green and its bunkers can still be seen. This was the third hole from the original course.

Third hole—Par 3—123 yards—The tee box for the third was located to the left of the second green. This was a short, simple, straightforward par 3, along the line of trees, and the site of the first hole-in-one for Charlie Murphy, who would later go on to win the State Mid-Amateur. This was the fourth hole from the original course. A note for winter walkers and skiers: there's a nice wooded trail that begins to the right of the old third green.

Fourth hole—Par 4—282 yards—The tee for the fourth hole was to the left of the old third green. This was a short par 4 that continued along the line of forest to the right. The green was located on a plateau behind the tee of the current Capital Hills course fourth hole. The outline of the green can still be seen. This is the original fifth hole.

Fifth hole—Par 4—382 yards—The tee box for the fifth hole was near the forward tee of the current Capital Hills fourth hole. Its remains, a slight mounding to the left of the cart path, can still be seen. At 382 yards, it was one of the longer par 4 on the course, and the fairway followed the line of trees that edge along the current third hole of the course. The hole played back across the current third fairway and beyond the current second green. The green was situated beyond the current second hole's green, near a newly planted tree. This was the original 14th hole.

Sixth hole—Par 3—167 yards—It's easy to see the remnants of the old sixth hole tee. A fading yellow tee marker and concrete benches are still tucked into the brush on the hill. The yellow hand rails leading down into the gully are also intact. This par three was the first taste of old Albany Muny golf, a shot over a chasm to a plateau green perched on the hillside. A beautiful hole, if you think about it, but that gully captured many a topped drive. This was the old 15th hole.

The Rev. Rand Peabody, who eulogized the passing of the old course in a 1991 essay in the *Times Union's* Perspective section, said the sixth would live on, at least in his memory. "As shots that had always been so real are relegated to the phantasms of memory, I will, of a winter's night, still feel the thrill of a ball dropping on a summery wind from the Helderbergs onto the shelf of the sixth green," he wrote.

Seventh hole—Par 4—278 yards—Walk off the green toward the woods and you'll find the familiar yellow hand rail leading you to the seventh hole. The seventh was a short but deceptive par 4 to another plateau green. Second shots to the left or right rolled off into a no man's land. With a straight shot and a sun-baked fairway, the green was drivable, but there was very little room for error, especially on the right. This was the original 16th hole, pulling golfers again toward the clubhouse. You'll see the tee for the eighth hole to your right as you walk up the fairway towards the green.

Eighth hole—Par 3—179 yards—Somewhere in the annals of golf writing, this hole should be marked up as equal to Augusta's 12th or the 17th at TPC Sawgrass—a fearsome par three. The only two-tiered green on the course, it bedeviled duffer and scratch golfer alike. Land short of the green and your ball could roll down the fronting hill. Hit right and you're stymied by a Norway maple that guards its side. This hole, which served as the original 17th, was the one true masterwork of Melville's original design. A bunker to the right of the green was eliminated in the 1950s. Walk off the back of the green and you'll be heading toward the tee box of the ninth hole.

Ninth hole—Par 5—463 yards—After the trials of the eighth, here was a breather coming back toward the clubhouse: a short par 5 with a tall elm tree guarding the right side of the fairway. A large green was positioned at the site of the current practice green, beyond the driving range, and at one point was surrounded by three spacious bunkers. This was the 18th hole of the original course. The ninth hole also was a prime spot to get beaned by errant drives off the 10th tee. A slice off the 10th would frequently curve into the ninth fairway.

Tenth hole—Par 4—361 yards—On the back nine, this was the only hole that withstood any changes from the original routing. The tee box was located near the site of the current maintenance shed and the green was located beyond the left side of the driving range. A straightforward par 4 with a bunker to the left of the green. Balls that hooked to the left were trouble.

Eleventh hole—Par 3—175 yards—A new par 3 created in 1949, the tee for the 11th was located on a plateau to the right of the tenth tee. Your tee shot crossed a valley to a green located where the course's maintenance crew now dumps debris, beyond the driving range. The hole was basically shoehorned in between what were the original 10th and 11th holes. Outlines of bunkers can still be seen near the old green.

Twelfth hole—Par 4—330 yards—The 12th hole was the original 11th hole, but it was shortened by approximately 60 yards. A short walk to the right of the 11th green and the tee was located to the right of the medium-sized maple tree. Tee markers and benches are still there for this straightaway par 4. Players shot down an undulating valley to a green guarded by several bunkers. Turn to the right off the green and you're heading to the tee for 13, the first of the four holes that criss-crossed Muny's notorious ravines.

Thirteenth hole—Par 3—125 yards—A short, easy par 3 which cut back across the right ravine. From the 12th green, walk right toward the wood line and you'll find the tee marker. Another hand rail hole. The 13th was the original 12th hole.

Fourteenth hole—Par 4—273 yards—Walk off the left of the green about 50 yards and you'll find the remains of the 14th tee, another yellow tee marker. The 14th continued across the next ravine and long hitters could frequently drive the green on this short par 4. Shots that came up short however, often left the golfer with an almost vertical approach shot. This was the original hole 13, and brought golfers back to the area where the current third green is located.

Fifteenth hole—Par 4—343 yards—Turning back across the ravines, golfers were in for a little more cardiovascular exercise. The tee was located near the former fifth green, as this served as the original sixth. Good drives on the 15th landed on the bank of a hill and golfers often had another awkward stance for their approach shot. "The 15th became the seminal hole for whether or not you were a long hitter," remembers Charlie Murphy. "Tommy Venter could drive that and I couldn't. He was a tall lanky kid with a beautiful swing. He could figure out how to drive it. We would hit it almost there and then it would roll back down to the first shelf."

Sixteenth hole—Par 4—280 yards—Behind the 15th green, the tee for the 16th continued you again across the gullies. Another hole where awkward lies were the rule, the green for the 16th was located around the corner from the 12th green. Frequently, players who had no desire for climbing the hills of 13–16, would chip over from the 12th hole and just play in 17 and 18, thus avoiding a lot of heavy breathing. This hole was played as the original seventh hole.

During the late 50s and early 60s, the 16th also became infamous for another reason. "We used to stand to the right of the green and hit balls over the creek to Normanside (Country Club). We did that a lot," remembers Mike Daniels. "We could reach the green over there. The trees obviously have grown in a lot over the years. Of course we wouldn't do it when people were on the green."

Seventeenth hole—Par 5—487 yards—Down a yellow hand rail now choked by overgrowth, players crossed the maintenance road to the 17th, which follows roughly the same fairway as the current eighth hole. The 17th's slanted fairway was tough to hold, especially in the dry summer months, and drew balls down to the right. The green was located beyond the current eighth green. The only par 5 on the back nine, this played as the original eighth hole.

Eighteenth hole—Par 4—388 yards—To the right of the 17th green, a path led down through the grove of trees and toward the tee of the finishing hole. The tee was located below the tees for the current 18th hole, and players drove out toward today's practice green, which served as the 18th green. When the course was re-done in 1989, the state DEC mandated that the green be raised about six inches to cover traces of chemicals from earlier pesticide applications.

The New Course at Albany (Capital Hills)—The area encompassing the first four holes of the new course is essentially the area used in the first designs. Only the layouts were amended. With holes five, six and seven, course architects Ed Bosse and Bob Smith moved into virgin territory along the banks of the Normanskill, and then turned again toward territory formerly used for the golf course. The back nine was a different story. Breaking new ground to the east of the old course, Bosse and Smith carved holes along the tract of land that paralleled the Thruway and then turned again toward the Normanskill.

"It is a 6,200-yard golf course that can make you play 7,000 yards," said former head pro Tom Vidulich. "You look at it and you think you should birdie every hole, but you don't."

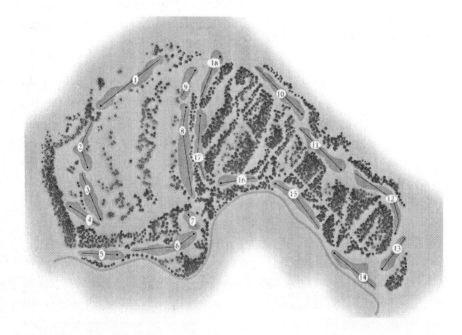

First hole (Old One)—Par 5—513 yards—The only hole that remained when Bosse and Smith made their overhaul in the late 1980s. The green was pushed back about 75 yards from the original design and additional tee areas were added throughout the decade of the

1990s. Bosse said he'd like to see the fairway landing area shaved down and leveled off a bit. The same could be done for the area in front of the green, he said, which would improve the sight lines to a somewhat blind green.

Second hole (Crimson Bend)—Par 4—335 yards—A short dogleg par 4. Bosse said the mandate from Mayor Whalen was to make a course that could be accessible for the average golfer—one that wouldn't be unduly difficult but tough enough for lower handicap players. "That's why you don't see any bunkers off the tee. Fairway bunkers can slow up play," said Bosse. The mounding that surrounds the green is reminiscent of Scottish links, and it was an element the design pair wanted to include in several of the holes.

"The green is always firm and fast front to back on the putting surface," said Vidulich.

Third hole (Pine Tree)—Par 4—360 yards—Another short par 4, but with a green that makes it easy to three-putt. "Three was kind of a nothing hole, pretty much a straight away but you had that potato chip green, and you really had to hit the right kind of shot to hold the green," Vidulich said. "You always felt you got screwed on that because you could hit a good shot and if it was in the back, you'd have a difficult two-putt. A simple little hole that played tough."

Bosse said the third could probably benefit from more, and higher, mounding along the edge of the fairway. Higher mounds would also bring more definition to the fairway and rough.

Fourth hole (Sand Pit)—Par 3—170 yards—"A great little par 3, well bunkered. Three is always a good score there," said Vidulich. An oak once guarded the left edge of the green, but was taken out in the mid 1990s. On the wish list is a plan to shave down the cart path hill heading toward the fifth hole to give a better view of the fourth green from the tee. Bosse said he and Smith had had to stay within budget parameters when completing the renovation, and earth moving is one of the more costly expenses of golf course construction.

"There were a couple of things we really wanted to do but the money just wasn't there for it," he said. "We wanted to utilize what nature gave us, but you're never finished with golf courses. There's always something you can do to make it better."

Fifth hole (Norman's View)—Par 4—285 yards—Bosse harkened again to his interest in Scottish links course design on the fifth, a hole he calls his favorite on the course. A small runoff ditch (in Scotland it might be called a "burn") winds across and along the right edge of the fairway. It solved a potential drainage problem and presents an honest hazard on the shortest par 4 on the course. The designers said they hoped to push the tee boxes further back but the land along the creek slopes down severely beyond the current blue tees.

As pro for ten years, Vidulich saw the potential downside of a short par 4—people trying to drive the green and creating backups at the tee. He had an altogether different idea for the fifth, a hole that people seem to either love or hate. "One year we had a tremendous amount of flooding. The creek overflowed and it created a natural island green at the fifth. It looked great and I always thought it was possible to recreate naturally," said Vidulich. "It would make it a true two-shot hole. Our backups always occurred there. People trying to drive the green, they wait till the hole clears and then all the sudden there's someone else waiting on the tee. If you make it a true island green, then you'd have to play two shots. It would take the driver out of your hand."

Sixth hole (One Pond)—Par 4—370 yards—Like its predecessor, the sixth hole runs along the Normanskill, but water comes into play even more on the sixth. A small reservoir, which fronts the left edge of the green, was created for the new course. It's the only true carry over water on the course.

An elevated tee was added in the early 1990s above the current tee boxes but the new tee never got much use. In 2001, it was covered in weeds, but it may be getting a second chance with recent renovations.

"When we put that tee up on top and it was in use, I always liked how the hole set up from there," said Vidulich. "Every time we had a meeting, that tee on the sixth would come up. There was a lot of finger pointing. The location is fine but somewhere in the construction, something happened."

Seventh hole (Tall Spruce)—Par 3—160 yards—"Seven's a great par 3," said Vidulich. "It plays tougher than it looks." Bunkers lined the back edge of the green on the uphill par three, but erosion from water coming down the hill constantly washed them out. They were difficult to drain, and eventually, they were removed. The wide thin green is a deceptively difficult landing area.

Eighth hole (Left Side Home)—Par 5—475 yards—"What makes the 8th a hard hole is not the fact that everything went to the right. It's very deceivingly uphill and the green was very long and narrow," said Vidulich. "You never seemed to take enough club to get it back there and you could hit the green and have a 70-foot putt. It's another one of those holes where if you look at it, it looked like a simple par five but there aren't a lot of birdies on that hole. If you do miss it right you're absolutely dead."

Bosse said the eighth hole took a good deal of earth moving. "It was very severely sloped from left to right and we leveled off a good amount of the fairway," he said. As most longtime Muny players will attest, the land occupying the eighth served as the 17th and, originally, the eighth hole on the old course. The tee was pushed back to create the short Capital Hills par 5.

Ninth hole (Easy Turn)—Par 3—180 yards—When the new course was first constructed, this hole was a 310-yard par 4. It also was the 18th, instead of the ninth hole. So many golfers complained about the original routing that the two holes were swapped. A year later, the new ninth hole was shortened from a par 4 to a par 3 and a new tee box was constructed further up the hill.

"We made the 9th the 18th hole partly because it seemed to flow better. Second, most of the guys that would play in the morning, they would leave the 8th hole and they wouldn't walk up the hill to nine. That's where people wanted it to be. And when you really put it together and looked at how the nines played, it made it a better finishing hole," said Vidulich. "In my view, the hole as a par four didn't set up well for anyone. When you stood on that tee as a higher handicap player, your view was nothing but woods, and every golf ball seemed to go there. As a more accomplished golfer, it just didn't have a good sight line. The hole was drivable. I remember getting Mayor Whalen out there and I drove him up in a cart to where the tee is now and I sat there with him and said it would be a great par 3, an amphitheatre effect, with the clubhouse in the background. People in the restaurant could watch people play this hole. This is a better par 3 than a par 4."

In years past, the small valley which houses the ninth hole served as one of the course's unofficial driving ranges. A bulls-eyed target green was located where the ninth green currently sits, and was used for many years when the *Times Union* held its hole-in-one contest at the course.

Tenth hole (Thruway Run)—Par 5—533 yards—The course takes its bend along the Thruway to start the back nine. "A solid par 5. The better player does need a little more length. I think they are planning on putting another tee up in back there," said Vidulich.

Bosse said the city had to negotiate with St. Sophia's Greek Orthodox Church, which owned part of the land that now makes up the tenth fairway. The land was purchased and the course continued along its Thruway run. The course designer said he'd like to see some moguls and mounding along the fairway to give the hole a little more definition.

Eleventh hole (The Valley)—Par 4—344 yards—A bit reminiscent of the old Albany Muny, and a good example of the kind of elevation changes the architects had to deal with, the 11th is more ski jump than golf hole. It's seen some subtle and not so subtle changes during the past 10 years.

"I don't know if you remember but there used to be a tree on the right. The tree died and it was taken down, so then it was just the sand on the left to guard the fairway," said Vidulich. "Well, that was Bob Smith's hole. He insisted that (course superintendent) Scott (Gallup) put a tree just right of the sand bunker. In the fairway. Oh my God, I had people coming to me absolutely screaming. So I said, 'Bob here's what I'm going to do with that tree. I'm going to take all your business cards and I'm going to staple them to the leaves of that tree. When they hit the tree with their drive they'll know who to call.' One day that tree mysteriously died and the cause of death is still undetermined."

If you can believe it, the valley of the 11th hole was actually about 30 feet deeper than it now appears. Bosse said the bottom was filled so that the slope was not so severe.

Twelfth hole (Oak Bend)—Par 5—492 yards—The two trees in the middle of the 12th fairway have stymied many a short hitter since the new course was constructed and the city recently added another tree between the two. Utilizing the landscape they had to work with, this should be considered one of Bosse and Smith's best additions to the new course. "Twelve was a lot of risk/reward," said Vidulich.

The open pastureland to the left of the 12th green is owned by the city and may someday be considered for golf course expansion.

Thirteenth hole (Mountain View)—Par 3—180 yards—A nice view of Normanside Country Club and the Helderbergs in the distance. Bosse and Smith were faced with another mammoth elevation change. Bosse said he initially wanted to run the hole so that it sloped more toward the 14th tee, making it a longer par 3.

"Thirteen was probably the only hole on the golf course that I didn't really care for. There wasn't much we could do to it. We looked around and there just wasn't much that we could do to make it a better hole," said Vidulich.

Fourteenth hole (Turning Home)—Par 4—398 yards—This hole was what Mayor Thomas Whalen envisioned when he set out to create the new course—a straightforward, reachable par 4 for the average golfer, and one that accentuates the natural beauty of the landscape, Bosse said. The 90-degree bend in the Normanskill near the tee box is a haven for wildlife. Ducks, herons and deer can be seen there on a regular basis, and it's a nice fishing spot as well. The hole follows the path of the Normanskill, and across the banks of the creek a sheer cliff reaches up some 300 feet. More tees were added here in the early 1990s to lengthen the hole slightly.

"This begins probably the best finishing holes anywhere around. I really believe that," said Vidulich. "That stretch of holes, from 14 through 18, has decided many city championships. If you could make pars coming in down the stretch on those holes, you were in good shape. You could hit good shots on those holes and still make bogies."

Fifteenth hole (Creek Side)—Par 4—420 yards—The longest par 4 on the course. A wide-open driving area allows long hitters to go for broke but everyone must negotiate a second shot into a well-placed green. Shots left can drop off into the gully that curls from the front to the left of the green. The hole also offers a nice stroll along the Normanskill and views of the 14th green and 15th hole at Normanside. Additional tee boxes were added in the early 1990s.

Bosse is justifiably proud of this and the 14th hole, which both demand a little more of the golfer. He said a bit more money during the construction process would have allowed a bunker to the left of the green here on the 15th. Once again, the landscape was shaved down to create a more level landing area.

Sixteenth hole (Double Dip)—Par 3—197 yards—Several tee boxes makes this the most adaptable par 3 on the course. From the tips, it can be a real challenge to hold a shot on the wide but narrow green. The original landscape was much more severely undulating. The hills were shaved down and the valleys filled to level the hole a bit. Another hole carved out of the forest along the water's edge.

Seventeenth hole (The Forest)—Par 4—406 yards—Since the New Course's first day of operation, the 17th has been considered its signature hole. It's justifiably the number one handicap hole and necessitates a solid well-placed drive and an approach shot to an elevated green. Drainage problems that left the fairway somewhat chewed up during much of the past decade have been solved, and the hole is a true test of par.

Eighteenth hole (Home At Last)—Par 4—361 yards—The practice area on the hill beyond the tennis courts was the original green for the home hole, but its slope and penal bunkers necessitated a change after the first two years of play. Even with excellent sand, the traps on the left side of the green and the deep swale on the right side were causing fits. Bosse said he initially wanted to create a "punch bowl" style green for the 18th. That would have meant moving several thousand tons of earth and it eventually proved too costly, especially because the Department of Environmental Conservation found the remnants of 40 years of chemical herbicides in the soil. The new green on the shelf to the right of the fairway was installed in 1995 and provides a more inviting target. It also frees up the putting/practice area. Bosse still calls the new green "temporary," but it's unlikely the old green will be utilized again.

Changes made in the summer of 2002 eliminated several trees to improve sight lines to the green. Some fairway bunkering also was added.

The Caddies

When the Albany Municipal Golf Course first opened its doors in 1932, caddies were a regular part of the golfing landscape. Within a few years of its opening, the course had a regular stable of bag toters, as well as a caddy shack located down the hill from the clubhouse. The shack would burn down in the late 1930s, but the caddy ranks would stay on through the early 1950s.

In the early years, the official going rate was 75 cents for a single bag, and $1.25 if you carried double, according to city records. The fee was halved for nine-hole loops, and caddies could make a few extra dimes shagging practice balls on the makeshift range below the old clubhouse.

According to newspaper accounts, more than 300 applied for positions as caddies when the course first opened, and of that number about 90 were picked. Not indicated was how many of those potential caddies were working men whose previous employment had dried up due to the depression. Even amongst the younger caddies, a good portion of the day's earnings often went to feed the family.

Several of the area's top amateur golfers, including 1944 State Amateur champ Joe Ruszas, came through the Muny caddy system. Caddying was indoctrination to the sport, and nearly all the top players from the early part of the century started out toting bags, many of them at Muny or the area's private clubs.

At age nine, Ed Huba began carrying bags out at Albany Country Club. "If you ever want to be a blackmailer, become a caddy," said Huba, with a laugh. "When you're out there walking right next to them for three or four hours, they will talk about anything. The things you hear will take your ears off. I always compared myself to being a slave because they didn't care if you heard what they were talking about or not."

Unlike most golf courses, the motorized golf cart wasn't the reason caddies faded from the scene at the Muny. Because of the severe hills golf carts were never allowed on the course. More than likely, the caddy system slowly died away because of simple economics. With the economy expanding after World War II, it became more difficult to find kids who wanted to carry bags for a buck or two, especially at the mountainous Albany Municipal. And while the course was as bargain basement as they come, golfers frequenting the Muny didn't feel the need to double their costs for the privilege of a caddy's company.

In the late 1930s, George Cinney was an impressionable young lad looking to enhance his family's income a bit.

George Cinney

A cold and clear September morning in 1939, and the golf season was winding down at Albany Muny. Outside the clubhouse, caddies gathered around a radio and listened to reports of an event that would soon change many of their young lives: Hitler had invaded Poland and Europe was spiraling into war.

"We were out there on the patio, and someone had a radio," remembers George Cinney. "Little did we know how many of us would wind up in service and some of us didn't make it back. We were listening very intently because probably 40 percent of our guys were Polish. Their parents were all immigrants."

In less than five years, Cinney would find himself patrolling the Pacific on the U.S.S. Houston with thoughts of the Muny hills far behind him, but he admits his caddy days opened his innocent eyes to a few things.

"It was an interesting time in my life because I was a young kid, just 12 when I started, and all ears," he said. "All of the other caddies were older than me. I learned a lot. I learned how to swear and a few other things my mother didn't know about."

In the process of learning a few choice phrases, Cinney didn't lack ambition. On summer days, he'd get the 5 a.m. bus from Dudley Heights, near Arbor Hill, and be at the club before 6 a.m.

"You were more or less assured of a job if you got your name in before 6 a.m. If you were lucky you'd get two loops in a day," he said.

With the Depression still making jobs scarce, the late 1930s caddy crew at Albany Municipal was a mixed bag of older men and strong-legged boys.

"There were married men caddying and us boys. I remember a guy named Yitz, Coberski, Zumbo, Bill Franks, John and Peter Cassera, 'Red' Crowder and Chuck Miller, who was killed at Guadalcanal. A great mixture of people, working men and teenagers. We had Italians, Poles. I remember I used to swap my peanut butter and jelly sandwich with some of the Italian caddies. They had roasted peppers."

With a dozen or more caddies waiting to carry, Cinney and his pals sometimes would go the extra mile to get a bag. "When Normanside had a tournament, they were always short of caddies. They would call over to Jerry Dwyer and ask if we had any caddies," he remembers. "We used to swim across the creek. There was a little raft we used to use and somebody would push that across with the clothes on it. We'd get dressed on the other shore and then go caddy."

The Arbor Hill kid made it through the battles in the Pacific, raised a family and went into the sales business, finally running his own food brokerage. He never caught the golfing bug as a kid but took up the game later in life. "Never really was much of a golfer," he said sheepishly. "My lowest score ever was a 75, at Albany Muny, with nine birdies, in a Class B event. With nine birdies you can imagine what I did on the other holes."

Most caddies have at least one good story about their time trudging the hills. Asked to recall his most memorable moment, Cinney tilts back his head with a knowing look that means a good one's coming.

"Had this fella on what used be the old 12th hole and I think it became the sixth hole, par three about 135 yards. We come to that hole and this fella was a real hacker and he says to me, 'Whaddya think, caddy?' I said 'Maybe a four iron.' It would have been about an 8 iron for a good golfer. He says 'Give me the driver.' He hit the best drive he hit all day. It flies up beyond the green, hits the top of a tree. The ball bounces off the tree down through the woods, through the rough, across the green and into the hole. He turns to me with a look that says, 'See I knew it was a driver.' It was the first hole-in-one I ever saw."

Tom Patterson (not the same Tom Patterson who was Jerry Dwyer's grandson) was probably among the last generation of Albany Municipal caddies.

Tom Patterson

Tom Patterson never became too interested in golf, but you can't really blame him. For four years, he worked as a caddy at Albany Muny, toting bags across the hills of the Normanskill vale.

"When I carried doubles (two bags at the same time) I was worn to a frazzle after 18," he recalled. "Those hills on the back were like Tibet."

Patterson was just ten years old when he began caddying at Muny in 1949, and although the work was rough, the few dollars for a round was about equal to what he could make in a whole week delivering newspapers, another job he started the year before. "I was a big boy, but after all, I was only 10," he said.

Patterson lasted for another three years, showing up on summer mornings from his South End home to wait out his turn with the four or five others who had taken instruction from pro Jerry Dwyer.

Although the monetary rewards were relatively decent, caddying wasn't what you'd call guaranteed income. Tips were hit or miss, depending on the disposition of your golfer or how much beer he'd consumed during the round. "Sometimes you'd never get called all day. We would just hang out behind the building. I don't think Dwyer had much use for us—a bunch of 10- and 11-year-old kids."

Patterson also remembers the abuse some caddies took from their employers. "Some of those golfers, they did a lot of drinking, and it was a wonder they could get around the course themselves," he said. "Not all of them, but some weren't too good to their caddies."

At the dawn of the 1950s, caddying was beginning to fade into a lost art at municipal courses, but at private clubs it still flourished. Places like Albany Country Club had special instruction programs set up for their bag carriers. They had higher wages, and as one might expect at a country club, access to better tippers.

"As caddies go, we were on the bottom rung compared to the kids at the private clubs," he said.

On occasion, Patterson would accompany Muny golfers to the private courses for tournaments or special matches. What he found there was a hierarchy that often put him at the bottom of the caddyshack ladder. A couple of times he made the uptown trip to Albany Country Club with a golfer he remembers only as "Duke." The clearest recollection of those trips was that he got, "beat up for my troubles."

Patterson, who recently moved back to the city after living in Bethlehem for 30 years, recalls his caddying experience as a collection of youthful lessons learned. But unlike others who took up the game after toting someone else's bag, his time at Muny was purely in the service of making a few bucks…the hard way.

"Like I said, there weren't many ways for a ten-year-old to make five dollars in those days."

The Professionals

Carl Seka (1931–1932)

With golfers lining up at the first tee and the course operating at a nice profit, it's still a puzzle why the Albany Municipal Golf Course's first head pro, Carl Seka, only lasted a few years. Seka's slicked black hair and dark features were a contrast to his assistant, Bill Murphy, a wiry Irishman who was known more for his good nature than his golf game.

Seka was the brother of Joe Seka, a pro who played with a vacationing Mayor Thacher on one of his winter jaunts to south Florida. It seems clear that Seka, from Philmont, Penn., was hired because of his connection to Thacher, (earlier news articles had Joe taking the job) but back then, golf professionals were a transient sort—it's not a 9-to-5 job, and money was made almost exclusively through pro shop sales, club repair and lessons.

For whatever reason, Seka left the course within two years of taking the job. He was replaced by the man whose patient disposition and good-natured personality dominated the course for the next 35 years—Jerry Dwyer.

Dwyer inherited one of Seka's two original assistants—Murphy, a rail thin Irishman who is worth mentioning because he brings a sly chuckle to any old-timer who remembers him. Murphy had a penchant for the drink. Some say his favorite breakfast beverage was orange soda and gin.

Murphy came to the municipal course from Albany Country Club, where he was an assistant to Scottish-born pro Ed Fitzjohn. "He (Murphy) was a good man, but he had that one failing. He could play golf. He hit the ball very straight," remembers Ed Huba, who caddied for

Murphy as a nine-year-old, first-year caddy at Albany Country Club. "Murphy had an Indian girlfriend and she was a character. Many a time guys picked on Bill and she took care of them. She was a powerful woman."

Although his duties were unofficial at best, he continued to hang around the course for a few decades. Some remember him as a regular in the bar through the 1950s. Murphy died a relatively young man and by a rather unusual cause. He was riding a city bus and was about to get off when the bus stopped quickly. "As I understand it, he was thrown forward and he hit the token box," Huba said. "I guess he thought he was alright, but he died soon after that."

Fitzjohn, by the way, played in the first-ever professional golf tournament held in the United States, and lost to his brother Val in a sudden death finale. He also is known in golf club collecting circles, with his handmade woods, stamped "Fitzjohn," garnering top dollar. But we're getting off the subject—the next pro at Albany Muny—"the old pro" himself, Jerry Dwyer.

Jerry Dwyer (1933–1965)

They saluted the old man in style on June 17, 1963. Perhaps they knew it wouldn't be long before Jeremiah Thomas Dwyer was trading golf jokes with Saint Peter rather than the faithful down below.

More than 150 showed up for the testimonial dinner at the DeWitt Clinton Hotel downtown. Mayor Corning proclaimed Jerry Dwyer Day in the city. Speeches shared the old pro's warmth, humor and patience. Walter Hagen was there, sequestered in an upstairs suite and offering a private audience for the man whose name had become synonymous with Albany Muny. For more than 30 years, Jerry Dwyer saw golfers come and go, leagues rise and fall. His presence marked the change of seasons for Albany golfers—a hopeful voice in spring and a consoling shoulder when autumn winds blew cold.

Dwyer rose, and his speech, sketched in pencil on the back of a paper sheet, was a homily. "It is very difficult for me to express my appreciation, trying to say just two simple words, thank you. A man is lucky if he has one friend. Tonight, I am surrounded by friends, real friends. You have made me very happy and very proud and I am extremely grateful. This is one night the old pro will never forget."

When a lifetimes' worth of cigarettes finally killed Jerry Dwyer at age 72, he had fulfilled a promise of sorts. He had made golf his life, taught thousands a love of the game and sealed an enduring legend. For many, the man they called "the old pro" *was* Albany Muny.

The Dwyers were Albany Irish root stock: a turn-of-the-century first generation family on Washington Avenue. The first Jeremiah Dwyer and the former Katherine Mulrooney had three boys, Jerry, Jimmy and John, and two girls, Margaret and Marie. All three boys were schooled in the caddy ranks at Albany Country Club. All three were considered prodigies and eventually became golf professionals.

Johnny was the natural athlete—a star on the Albany High School basketball team and a scratch golfer within a few years of taking up the game. Just past his teen years, charming and friendly Johnny was asked to become the pro at the new Stanford Golf Club out near Schenectady. From there he moved to Mechanicville Country Club, and began establishing himself as one of the top young pros in the Northeast. When Hagen and soon-to-be inaugural Masters tourney champ Horton Smith arrived in Albany on a barnstorming tour in the late 1920s, it was Johnny and Jerry Dwyer who took them on. The matches, eventually won by Hagen and Smith, drew a stampede of fans to the Roost's fairways.

"Johnny was the one they always said was the real athlete in the family," remembers Jerry's daughter, Geraldine Zwack. "He was a star basketball player and a great golfer."

At age 25, Johnny Dwyer held the scoring record for his home course, a handful of Northeastern New York PGA trophies and the promise of solid professional career, if not national prominence.

Then, he got sick. It was nothing, really—a sore tooth. Today, a dose of penicillin would tackle it in days. But in the 1920s, an infected tooth could become pneumonia and meningitis. It did, and within two weeks, the golfing Dwyer boys had been reduced by one.

"Johnny's passing robs golf and the sports world in general of a colorful and lovable character," wrote a local columnist. "Death at its best is no respecter of persons, but it seems particularly cruel to strike down so gallant a figure on the very threshold of the goal he sought."

We can't know the effect their brother's death had on Jerry and Jimmy, but if golf was Johnny's life, they would continue to make it theirs as well.

Like their brother, the pair were already well entrenched in the local links scene. At the age of 17, Jerry had been hand picked by Albany Country Club pro Ed Fitzjohn to be an assistant, and the old Scot may have saved the boy from a life on the ropes. Up until his 16th year, young Dwyer had been undefeated in amateur boxing bouts at Albany's German Hall and he was leaning toward a career trading punches rather than swinging niblicks. The steady, if not spectacular, income from a full-time job at Albany CC convinced him that golf was a surer long-term career.

Dwyer moved on to Wolferts Roost and in a few years, he had accepted a post at Poland Country Club, just outside Youngstown, Ohio. His tenure as a head pro had begun. The Dwyer boys entered the field as it was beginning to gain some respect. Prior to Hagen and his colorful contemporaries, golf pros were often thought of as glorified caddies who happened to possess the necessary club repair skills to keep a golf shop afloat. The boom in private courses during the 1920s created a club professional who could multi-task—teach duffer and top amateur alike; mend and sell clubs; glad-hand the gentry; and make a few bucks at the fledgling "tour" events. In 1931, the U.S. Open was held at Inverness in Toledo, and for the first time, the few touring professionals were allowed in the clubhouse to use the locker room. Even to the country club set, golf professionals had finally become somewhat respectable.

By the time he had reached his late 20s, Jerry's career had taken him halfway across the country, and in competition against some of the best golfers in America. It wasn't a fluke that Hagen, probably the most recognizable pro of his time, made a special trip to Albany that night 40 years later. The two were old pals, and Jerry always considered the dapper "Haig" his idol.

While head professional at Poland, Dwyer achieved one of the rarest of golf's statistical feats during the 1924 Western Open—a double eagle 2 on what was the par 5 16th at Youngstown Country Club. It was to be his highlight reel as a pro—the one story he would recall when sportswriters came calling. But Jerry must have known he wasn't cut out for life on the road. His place was in a home club, and his real magic was on the lesson tee. Newly married to a Youngstown girl, Edna Landers, Dwyer returned to Albany and what seemed to be a plum position—head pro at Wolferts Roost Country Club.

Two years later, the stock market crash made golf courses seem like so much unused cow pasture and the Roost didn't look like such a sure thing after all. The club wasn't going under but it wasn't exactly thriving either. In 1933, with the Depression at its worst, Dwyer got the call that would set his future. He said "yes"; he would accept Mayor Thacher's request to become the new head pro at the Albany Municipal Golf Course. It was a step down from the Roost, perhaps, but the decision proved fitting.

"When the Depression came, people stopped playing and so he moved out to municipal, where he remained because he gave such marvelous lessons," said daughter, Gerry, who would come to be known by regulars as "the little pro." "He had so many lessons that he did well. We never wanted for anything. People loved him, they really did. He was a very genuine, kind fellow."

Thankfully, Jerry also was a patient man. He was fixated on golfing mechanics and the idea that a perfect swing was obtainable for just about everyone as long as they knew the fundamentals. Lessons were what kept Jerry and the family going through the next 40 years. Nearly

40,000 lessons by some count. What must have seemed an exhausting and frustrating task, Jerry always took up with acceptance and hope. During winter months for the next four decades, he would bring his lesson tee to Albany, Bethlehem and Guilderland high schools as well as local office buildings and factories. Anywhere he could set up a net and find a disciple, he would teach the swing.

"He was a real student of it. In the winter he used to have a little office upstairs. He was pretty good sketcher and he would sketch the mechanics of the swing, showing the proper position for the take away, the follow through. He would spend hours, weeks and months at it," said Tom Patterson, Jerry's grandson and pupil. "He was a true student of the swing."

In that upstairs office each winter Jerry puttered away on a series of golf inventions. If the infomercial were alive back in the 1950s, he might have made a million. One of Dwyer's most promising gadgets was aimed at helping pros custom fit clubs to their clientele. The "Dwyer Lie De-Tek-Tor" was marketed nationally to club pros two decades before Karsten Solheim and his friends at Ping caught on to the same concept.

A September 1938 article in the *Times Union* outlines one of Jerry's early inventions for helping the beginning golfer. He called it the "Golf Swing Post"—nothing more than a padded, adjustable headrest jutting out from a post. Jerry told the reporter, "The golfer puts his head in here, his ball directly below, and then leans his weight on the head piece and he's ready to practice his swing. It aids beginners to gain the proper balance. With his head in place, the golfer can concentrate fully on getting the proper shift of his weight."

If Dwyer made any money off the Golf Swing Post, Lie De-Tek-Tor or any of his other inventions, he didn't flaunt it. The family lived in a modest home on Betwood Street, a quick drive from the course. To the Dwyers, the pro shop was a family business. "My mother would always be helping him out in the shop and of course when we weren't in school, my sister Sally and I would be there as well," said Gerry Zwack.

"The little pro, that's what they called me. When I was in my teen years, we would take care of the pro shop when he was out giving lessons. It was a nice place to meet boys."

While Dwyer became known as a tireless tutor of the game, he also was a pretty fair player. On July 18, 1938, he set out for what would prove to be his low round at the Muny course, and the best round ever for the course's original 18-hole layout. Out in 33, with birdies at the first, third, fifth and eighth holes, only a bogey at the ninth would mar his scorecard. On the par-35 back nine, he strung together birds at holes 13, 14 and 16, and then laced up the record with an eagle three at the 507-yard 18th. A 63 on the par 72 course. Although the layout would be changed and re-routed in 1949, Dwyer's scorecard, framed and illustrated, would hang in the pro shop until his passing. His record round was never touched.

Most golfers don't realize that club pros rarely get the opportunity to play 18 holes during the season. With the pro shop and a full lesson schedule there's just too many other demands on their time. For someone whose income was greatly reduced during the winter months, Dwyer had to make his money from April through September, and that kept him, as the old sportswriters would say, "as busy as a one-armed paper hanger." With help in the shop from his wife and two daughters, Dwyer got out when he could, especially in his later years. Jerry would compete in NENY PGA events and he still could hang with the young pros. "Even at 68, 69, he had a terrific swing," said his grandson, a frequent playing partner. "Sometimes I would caddy for him in the Monday matches against other pros. He was still breaking 80, not making any bad shots."

While he had time for nearly everyone who wished to learn the game, one of the hallmarks of Dwyer's career was his work with blind golfers. Following World War II, hundreds of vets returned sightless from the war and golf was one of the few athletic endeavors they could take up. Dwyer not only helped establish Chapter Two of the Middle Atlantic Blind Golfers Association, but also guided dozens of blind

men and women into the game. He established caddy assistant programs for the sightless, and one of those schooled in the program was
Patterson.

"A lot of the fellows were wounded in World War II and lost their
sight, a few had played before, some had never played before," said
Patterson. "He'd organize myself and the other kids to be their caddies,
showed us how to do that. We'd have to tee the ball up and line them
up and tell them how far. Some of those guys shot respectable scores,
high 80s, low 90s. You can imagine how tough that would be. They
loved it when they got a par."

In a sports page obituary a day after Dwyer's death, John Dillon,
president of the Blind Golfers Association's local chapter, was quoted.
"Jerry did more than any other man for our players, giving up hour
after hour to help their games. There is a big empty space in the blind
golfer's world today."

Jerry Dwyer never retired. As he lay in a hospital bed that summer
of 1965, the Albany Muni team brought home another Northeastern
Junior Golf League divisional championship. Playing against sons of
privilege, the muny kids swept through undefeated, topping Schuyler
Meadows, 15–0, for the title.

"I remember him as a wonderful man, very helpful, genuine and
laid back," remembers Mike Daniels, one of the junior golfers who
were tearing up the course for the Muny team. "He had a marvelous
personality and he was always there with advice when you needed it."

In the end, that's how the old pro wanted to be remembered.

Bob Moore/Jim Gradoni/Ted Rau (1966–1990)

The passing of Jerry Dwyer left the city fathers with a decision. They
could find another pro to fill his shoes or run the course with a manager acting as unofficial "pro." Perhaps the shoes were a bit too large to
fill. They chose the latter.

For the next 25 years, the Albany Municipal Golf Course was without a registered PGA professional, and the course suffered in both real-

ity and reputation. But the men who ran the golf shop, starting with Bob Moore in 1966, had a close connection to the course, and many a golfer can credit Moore and Ted Rau for teaching them the basics of the game. Neither had the credential to call themselves "professionals," but both were top amateurs and had a muny heritage years before they took over the unofficial pro position.

Moore came from a family of three brothers, all of whom played the course during their lifetime. Brother Jack worked for the railroad, and Ned worked for the federal government in a variety of roles. Newspaper reports said he was an electronics engineer.

"Everybody assumed, and he did not try to squelch the rumor, that Ned worked for the CIA. He was in Vietnam in the very early 1960s," said Charlie Murphy, who worked in the clubhouse under Bob Moore during his teenage years.

Brother Ned qualified for the 1950 US Open at Oakmont, carding a 71 in the first round. In a 1973 *Times Union* "Where are they now?" piece, he was recalled as a "Nicklaus-style" long-ball hitter who even played in the Korean National Amateur Championship, while serving there in the late 1950s. He reached the finals in 1958, only to be beaten out by U.S. Army General George Decker, the article noted.

Bob, not the equal to his brother but a pretty decent golfer himself, had a career with the Niagara Mohawk Power Company before taking over behind the pro shop counter. All three Moore brothers were said to be fine golfers and also fine drinkers. Murphy recalls arriving at work one pre-dawn morning to discover Bob reclining comfortably on the floor behind the pro shop desk. "I honestly thought he was dead for a minute," he said. "Bob was a definitely an old fashioned pro. He had a good time in the bar, if you know what I mean."

Moore and his brothers were caddies at Albany Muny in the 1930s, and Murphy recalled one of their often-told tales. "They had some Korean businessmen who came out to play golf at the Muny and they would always elaborate the story with the Asian accents. They took these guys out and they claim they took them out back to the 16th hole and took them down the hill, put them on a boat or something, rowed over to Normanside, played 18 holes at Normanside and then came back and played the Muny. They said these guys were so impressed. '36 holes in one day with a boat to the other 18!!!' The caddies got a huge tip because these rich Korean businessmen had never seen a course that had a boat ride in the middle of it."

James Gradoni followed Moore in the mid 1970s, but was only to stay at the Muny for a few years. Another teaching pro without PGA certification, Gradoni at one time worked as a course manager for the Watervliet Arsenal's pitch and putt course. The Cohoes native most likely came to Albany Muny from a driving range job out on Route 7, said his cousin John Gradoni. "He was a teaching pro at a driving range out there past Howard Johnsons. I remember taking my sons out there for lessons so that must have been 35 years ago," John said.

Gradoni left Albany Muny after just two or three years and later worked at the Stadium Golf Course in Schenectady, where he was known to give free clinics to junior golfers on Saturday mornings. Ironically, his cousin John Gradoni also considered becoming a golf professional. John was a protégé of longtime Van Schaick professional Johnny Gaucas, but the Korean War interrupted his links plans. "I came back from the war and then got married and golf wasn't so important anymore," he said.

Ted Rau also had a Muny heritage. The inaugural Eastern New York Golf Association Publinks titleholder in 1940, Rau grew up playing at Albany Muny but also played for several years out of the now defunct nine-hole Stanford Golf Club in Schenectady.

"He was the self-proclaimed pro, but he taught me how to play," remembers Eagle Crest pro Jim Jeffers. "He really was the main influence on me getting into the golf business. It didn't make a difference who you were or how much money you made, he treated everyone the same. The nicest guy I ever met."

Perhaps a little too nice. Jeffers recalls that Ted used to leave the door to the pro shop open when he would go off to give a lesson or play a round, and often some unscrupulous golfers would steal him blind. "You'd walk in there and guys would be trying on shoes, filling up their pockets with golf balls. He probably gave away more stuff than he sold," he said. "I finally said to him, 'I'm here, why don't you let me watch the shop for you?' I guess that was my start in the golf business."

Jeffers said Ted also had the habit of giving two-hour golf lessons to the best looking women in Albany. "Everyone else would get a half hour or 20 minutes, but with the women, he would disappear on the back nine for a few hours."

Rau installed the first driving range at the course, which was housed near the maintenance shed. He also had the only golf cart on the course for many years, a three-wheel Harley Davidson, which had a habit getting stuck quite frequently on the back nine. "It was hilarious. We'd always go out there and help him get it unstuck," Jeffers said.

When the city fathers finally decided to revamp the old course in the late 1980s, Ted wanted to stay on, but without designation as a PGA-certified professional his time was numbered. He moved on to Eagle Crest for two years, and then moved out to Arizona. "The guy had more energy at 75 than I had at half his age," recalled his successor, Tom Vidulich. "I'm not surprised that he kept teaching."

According to Jeffers, Ted was still giving lessons into his 90s. He died in 2001. "From what I heard, he was giving lessons two days before he died. He was just a regular guy, but one of a kind. Ted took everyone at face value."

Tom Vidulich (1991–2001)

By his own estimation, Tom Vidulich was not a popular man when he first arrived at Albany Muny in 1991. For more than 10 years, Ted Rau had run the golf course with a casual hand and a large contingent of friends. The place was comfortable and homey, but as a golf course, it was a wreck. Tee boxes were nothing more than dirt pads, bunkers were neglected. Not that the derelict course was Rau's fault, but for several decades, the Muny had floated in the backwash of the city's consciousness and stabilized its reputation as a goat track.

With the swipe of a pen and a few million dollars, Mayor Thomas Whalen changed all that, and now the man who was Whalen's appointed "new pro" for the "New Course" had a tough job on his hands—move the course forward but bring the faithful along.

"I knew Ted, played some golf with him, because he was around during that transition period that first year. You know, it was kind of an awkward time. I certainly didn't have any control over his transition there," Vidulich said. "You can't blame the people who may have been unhappy about what happened, and Ted had his friends. It was an uncomfortable time. You had to walk that very fine line and try to not to offend anyone, which is impossible."

Vidulich's job was to be the new face of a new course, to shift the impression of a rundown muny to a potentially top-flight public course. That meant no tank tops. That meant *everyone* had to make a tee time. That meant he had to say "no" to a few people.

On the day he was officially hired by the city, the new head pro sat down with course superintendent Scott Gallup and the two brainstormed about what the course could become. Their goals were lofty. "We both sort of had a goal that we wanted to follow, and that was to be the best public golf course, anywhere. We never deviated from that goal. We always did what we thought was best for the golf course and not what was best for us. I'm very proud of that and I miss working with him because of that," Vidulich said.

The Amsterdam native came to the Muny job through persistence. Although he didn't know the mayor personally, Vidulich said he lobbied hard for the job. "I guess you could say I stalked him for a while," he said with a laugh. "Every place he was, I was. I called everybody I knew who knew him. I was seven years at the Roost and there weren't a lot of opportunities opening up. It seemed like when they did, they would go with someone from outside the area. If there was something that had any glimmer of hope, you pounced on it."

Although he had been golfing since childhood and had caddied at the Antlers, the sport definitely was not Vidulich's first career choice. In his late 20s, he was working at the State University system administration when he decided to restart his life. Law school and a career as a physical therapist were fleeting options but several of his friends were golf professionals and they convinced him to give it a try. "I figured I might as well do something I really like," he said.

Vidulich got lucky. His first assistant position was under the tutelage of longtime Wolferts Roost pro Bob Smith, a man Vidulich calls "the greatest golf pro in the world" and "one of the toughest sons of bitches I've ever met" in the same breath. "My career was always based on one simple thought, that if I could learn half the things that Bob Smith has forgotten, I'd be a good pro," he said.

Smith as mentor may have had a little to do with Vidulich becoming pro at the newly named New Course at Albany. He and former Colonie pro Ed Bosse were hired by the city to do the layout of the course reconstruction. Vidulich's persistent lobbying for the job and his connection to Smith were obviously influencing factors. "I interviewed for the job. I know there were a few others who interviewed. Personally, I thought the interview went horrible, but a couple of weeks later, I got a letter," he said.

For the next ten years, Vidulich, Gallup and company followed their goal of making the new muny the best public track in the area. The course, which opened to generally favorable reviews, was tweaked and amended. From the sheer number of golfers teeing up each summer, it was a financial success, but Vidulich said that some unpopular decisions were made throughout his tenure. Some he could control, but most he couldn't.

In 1999, for example, season fees were hiked and the Friday night leagues were told they had to fold to make way for non-league players. It was a financial decision, not made by Vidulich, which turned into a bad PR move. But guess who got all the grief? "That was another one of those times when I wish I had gotten out of town more often," Vidulich said.

After ten years at the New Course, Vidulich moved on. In 2001, he opened the North Country Golf Academy in Plattsburgh. "Well, I had ten great years there and it was time to do something different. I came up here where I knew the weather was going to be horrible. We have an indoor golf facility with simulators, indoor range, teaching, club fitting, retail sales, beer, wine, food, beverage," he said. "It's different and it's challenging. I do an awful lot of teaching, which I had really gotten out of down there because I never had the time. This place allows me to be more of a golf pro and less of an administrator."

Vidulich has scant memory of the "old course" at Albany. When he arrived the focus was on the new 18 holes about to open. "I never saw that course in its heyday. I saw it in its post-construction, lack of interest period. From photographs I've seen of the old course, I'm sure it had a lot of character. What I saw was sort of a white elephant, and I wondered how people played it. I mean, the front nine wasn't so bad. I played the back nine and went home and slept for a week I was so exhausted. It was like climbing mountains."

The Clubhouse

"After every Election Day, she would come striding in (to the clubhouse), and she was the nicest person, but it was like she was the queen. You'd hear people say, 'Mary Marcy's coming. Mary Marcy's coming.' And boy when she came in, she just swept into the room. It was like out of a storybook. But here we were in this old clubhouse. They'd be out on the porch with a keg of beer and cakes for the ladies. It was so down to earth that place. It was like being home when you were there."

Much has already been written about the decades-long benevolent dictatorship known as the Corning Years, but at humble Albany Muny, the powerful few often mingled comfortably with those who buttered their bread. Without question, the Muny course was for decades a haven of patronage jobs, handed out to loyal voters. While many city employees throughout the years did work to keep the course in playable condition (city reports boasted, "all mowed fairways, eliminating all rough," for the "finest and sportiest golf links in this area") many others simply showed up on the Fridays the weekly cash payments were handed out. According to those who witnessed the weekly ritual, the municipal golf course surely had its share of "no show" employees.

This was, after all, Democratic Albany's tried and true system for keeping the mayor in City Hall, and one of those instrumental in arranging such positions was Mary Marcy, mentioned above. For nearly her entire adult life, Mary handed out jobs for city voters of the right political persuasion, and the Albany Municipal Golf Course was a fine place for those in need of employment.

Mary, whose son, Mickey, ran the clubhouse bar for more than 20 years, was appointed second vice chairman of the Albany County Democratic Party in 1928. She held the same powerful post nearly 60 years later when she died in 1987, less than a week before her 100th birthday. Mary was considered one of the most loyal and hard-working members of the party's upper echelon, and getting in her good graces could mean a job in your future.

With Mickey working behind the bar and the Hedrick beer flowing, the clubhouse at the municipal course became a home away from home for countless men, whether on the payroll or not. They were men hiding from their wives, men hiding in a bottle, men just looking for a little conversation, or all of the above. Their common denominator was an unshakeable allegiance to the Democratic Party, and for decades the tavern itself became an adjunct party headquarters.

Fresh out of high school in the early 1960s, three-time city champ Joe Rafferty worked behind the bar for three years with Mickey and his brother, Bill Marcy. "When I turned 18, a guy quit there so Mickey asked if I wanted the job. I worked there for about two summers before I went into the fire department," Rafferty said.

Rafferty confirmed the idea that the clubhouse bar was often a hangout for the Albany Democratic Party's power elite. He has nothing but fond memories of former Mayor Erastus Corning, whom he often accompanied on hunting and fishing trips to the Adirondacks. "After the Democratic party meetings at the Polish hall, they used to come in to the (golf course) bar. Jimmy Ryan, Charlie Ryan, Mary Marcy, the Mayor and Polly Noonan. They'd sit there and have a beer and some cheese and crackers, but you could tell they were there for more than just cheese and crackers. They were probably discussing what went on at the meeting."

While Rafferty was tending bar, another longtime Muny golfer was making a few extra bucks at the course. Charlie Murphy began working at the course as a 16-year-old in 1963 and eventually moved to jobs on the grounds crew and in the bar. By then, Jack McCaffrey had taken over the establishment. "You got paid in a white envelope, and full-time employees got paid $30.39 a week. 75 cents an hour. There was no minimum wage we were told because it was a city job. For many years we were seasonal and then when I was in college we were year round. In the winter, we would literally be watchmen. I remember we painted the clubhouse one year. I was here the Sunday that Jack Ruby shot Lee Harvey Oswald. I used to bring my television in because there wasn't much activity here in November."

Murphy and Rafferty were two who actually worked for their wages, but the former remembers a string of "course employees" who would suddenly appear on the days the white envelopes were handed out. "On the cashier side, to cover all the shifts there were probably four or five of us, and on the course, 10 or 12, but on Fridays, 50 people would show up. Widows would show up for dead guys, and it was cash in an envelope—$30.39."

Murphy also remembers a *Times Union* expose during the mid-1960s, which intimated that not everyone employed at the golf course was working a full shift. "They had my name in the paper and my mother went crazy," he remembers. "The city had some sort of answer, but I don't think it satisfied the paper."

Even after he joined Pinehaven and Albany Country Club, Murphy continued to work behind the bar at Albany Muny. What kept him there? The place was just a hell of a lot of fun. "One time, Jimmy McCaffrey walked out of the kitchen covered with ketchup and he said, 'The grill's exploded.' He would make everybody laugh.

"There was no place like it," he said. "It was a golf course, but there was so much more to this place than golf. There was a cast of characters here that hung out at the bar. When Jack ran this place it was an honest to goodness gin mill. There were doctors, lawyers, real estate guys, businessmen and they were a colorful bunch."

Patronage jobs at the muny course followed the pattern of change as a new guard of politicians vied for power through the 1980s. In 1987, the *Times Union* again found the course fodder for an expose. It ran a series of stories on the unusual work hours of then-course manager Robert Mahar, which alleged that Mahar was being paid more than $17,000 for his city job, when he also held down a $40,000-a-year position with the state.

A First Ward Democratic committeeman, Mahar countered that he worked early mornings, late afternoons and weekends for his city pay. "The bulk of our business is the leagues in the evening and the weekends," he was quoted as saying. Within a week of the story breaking, he had resigned the golf course job, and replaced by the course foreman, Walter Johnson, another former Democratic committeeman from the city's First Ward.

The *Times Union* stories went on to outline the overwhelming number of First Warders in employ at the golf course. In May 1987, nine out of 11 full-time employees on the golf course payroll were from the South End ward. Not only were nearly all the employees neighbors, a few were neighbors and relatives, as well. The newspaper traced the hiring trend back to former city Department of Public Works chief Harry Maikels, whose department once oversaw the course for many years. Maikels allegedly used his position as ward leader and DPW chief to dole out jobs to friends.

But with the death of Mayor Corning and the rise of new leadership in the city, the patronage system had begun to slowly ebb away. The bar remained the same—a dark, little establishment sent from a different place and time. For a youngster coming in after a day of wholesome sledding during the winter, it was a stark introduction. This is what a real bar looks like, kid.

When they tore the old place down, the rubble sat for a week or so, and a few old timers came by to pay their respects. Sure, the new bar is bigger, and the food is probably much better, but the old place had a history all to itself. Just ask anyone who spent some time there.

The New Course

It's been said that guilt and shame were the impetus behind the expansive South Mall project that changed the face of downtown Albany. When Mayor Corning and Governor Nelson Rockefeller hosted Princess Beatrix from the Netherlands on a 1960s visit, Rocky looked around the once vibrant city, and saw it with a realist's eye—rundown neighborhoods, a derelict shopping district, not the kind of place that bespeaks a capital city.

On a much smaller level, the same drive may have been responsible for the overhaul that reinvented the old course at Albany Municipal into the brand spanking "New Course at Albany."

Mayor Thomas Whalen was never less than an 18 handicapper, but he certainly loved golf and he wanted a course that his city could be proud of. The funds for a new course and Whalen's passion for the game came together in the late 1980s during his first full term as mayor.

"The place was an embarrassment, and it was embarrassing for the mayor to run a capital city with a course like this," said Richard Barrett, Whalen's parks and recreation chief. "(The mayor) was a Pine Hills kid who went to VI (Vincentian Institute) and grew up playing at the course, but he knew that it was inadequate and he knew that if a better facility could be created, it would be a big draw and a revenue generator for the city. The course was for billygoats and the clubhouse was basically a bar where a lot of old guys hung out. The city was probably barely making $100,000 annually. What's it making now? Probably half a million."

On top of the revenue, Whalen knew that a strong parks system in the city would go a long way to help stem the flow of middle class families out to the suburbs, Barrett said. "He understood that a nice, well maintained municipally-owned golf course is a strong draw and that it might make families stay in the city. He saw the success the Town of Colonie was having and he wanted the same for the city," Barrett said.

In the winter of 1987, the plan came together. Whalen announced that the city would use a portion of its $28 million budget surplus to create a "redesigned" Albany Municipal Golf Course. Specifically noted in Whalen's remarks were the holes of the old course's back nine, which the mayor simply called "unplayable."

Much like his mayoral predecessor John Boyd Thacher a half century before, Whalen assembled a team of staffers and consultants to move the project forward. The city's budget director Dan Klepak was as much a golf fanatic as his boss, and through his membership at Colonie Country Club, he knew Ed Bosse was in the final years of his pro career there. Whalen had long been friends with another well-tenured area professional, Bob Smith of Wolferts Roost Country Club, who also was nearing retirement. The pair signed on in 1987 as consultants to help redesign the course. That winter, Bosse said, he and Smith began roaming the course with maps in hand. The firm of Hershberg and Hershberg were chosen to provide the engineering work for the project and Clark Construction of Delhi would do the earthmoving.

"When this got moving, we met pretty much every week. The mayor was good at putting a task force together, and he wanted this to go," Barrett said.

The pair of newly-named course designers came of age, and came to golf in similar circumstances. Bosse started caddying as a youngster at Meadowbrook Country Club near Buffalo. Smith's family happened to live just off the second hole of Amsterdam Municipal Golf Course, only the second public golf course in the country built by Robert Trent Jones Sr.

Smith was about ten when he started caddying and teeing it up on a regular basis at Amsterdam Muny. He said he was never much into competitions as a youngster but challenged himself to get better. "One day I was caddying for the pro there, Jimmy Hines, and someone came out and said to Jimmy 'Your assistant just quit.' I guess that's when I became his assistant," he said.

Smith stayed at Amsterdam until 1951, when he took the head pro job at Cobleskill. He lasted just a year there when Wolferts Roost called in 1952. Nearly 40 years later, he was still the Roost's head pro, probably one of the longest stays at one course for any area professional.

"I'll tell you truthfully, I never had a bad day while I was there. The people were so good to me, I couldn't wait to get there and get to work each day," he said.

In the winter months, he worked for a time at Clearwater, Fla.'s Bellevue Biltmore course during the 1960s and early 1970s. Smith also spent several years as vice president of the national Professional Golfers Association—overseeing tournaments and officiating the Ryder Cup matches in 1983.

Bosse, likewise, started in the caddy ranks, and was a natural athlete as a youngster. After graduating from Cortland State, he returned soon after to coach its football team. "I always knew I wanted to be either a golf professional or a football coach. I got to do both," he said.

After three years on the sidelines, however, he saw a better future on the links. Bosse worked at Cold Spring Country Club on Long Island before taking the coaching job and when he left Cortland, he played for a time on the PGA and Caribbean PGA tours, staked by a few wealthy benefactors. He settled briefly as an assistant to Johnny Farrell at the Country Club of Florida, before returning to New York in the early 1960s. Bosse arrived at Colonie Country Club during its biggest transition, officially taking over as head pro the year before the club left its layout on the corner of Wolf Road and Central Avenue and moved out to New Scotland.

Like Smith, he has few regrets about his career path. "If I had it to do over again, I'd do it all the same," he said. "The members out there were great."

After a combined 70 years as club professionals, Bosse and Smith jumped at the chance to expand their repertoire into the field of course design, but aside from ongoing minor adjustments at their home clubs, neither had a lot of experience. In the late 1950s, Bosse had designed five holes at the Star Lake Inn golf course in the Adirondacks. More recently, he had attended golf course construction school under the tutelage of Tom Fazio and other notable designers. With his long tenure at the Roost, Smith had tinkered with the A.W. Tillinghast design there, modifying bunkers and reshaping some greens. But the expanse of city-owned land now presented to Bosse and Smith was a blank slate, ready for a new course to be carved from its rolling hills and creekside lowlands. The task ahead would take three years and the city would fight several public relations battles before the project was completed.

Whalen told the pair he wanted a course that would challenge a low handicapper but not one that would intimidate the average player. He also wanted Bosse and Smith to use the city-owned land bordering the Normanskill. Both were avid students of course architecture and with a lifetime spent walking around golf courses, they certainly knew what worked and what didn't. Smith said he wanted to follow the lead of Trent Jones Sr., whose credo was that every hole should be "a tough par but an easy bogey." Bosse had a particular love for the links courses of Scotland, and wanted to incorporate some of visual elements found there—mounding along the fairway edges, pot bunkers and small burns running through the course.

"Dan Klepak said to me, 'The mayor's going to ask if you can do this.' I said I could, and it happened," Bosse recalled. "He gave us free rein."

Smith had a closer relationship with the mayor, and he remembers Whalen's constant harangue during the early 1980s. "I'd see the mayor at different events and he would always be talking about the (municipal) golf course, saying 'We gotta take care of our constituents.' He asked if I'd go out and take a look at the course. I came back and said to him, 'They don't really play golf out there, do they?' It was the worst looking thing I'd ever seen," Smith said.

In the fraternity of local golf professionals, Smith and Bosse had been fast friends, but temperamentally they were polar opposites. The division of duties eventually became a sore subject. Smith became ill shortly after they began working on the project, and Bosse claims to have taken on most of the actual layout work. Smith said they often worked separately but the project was split fairly evenly. After a 1989 article in the *Times Union* quoted Bosse exclusively, Smith called him on the phone with a few choice words.

"We didn't talk for a couple of weeks but we finally kissed and made up. He's a stubborn son of a bitch," said Smith.

The silent partner in the design work was Daniel Hershberg, whose family firm was named the engineer in charge of the project. Early in his career, Hershberg had worked with course architect Geoffrey Cornish on the new Colonie Country Club layout, providing grading plans, technical drawings and some surveying work. With his practical experience and professional background, Hershberg, also a golfer, would become indispensable to the redesign project, injecting some practicality into the pros' suggestions. He even ended up designing the logo used for the New Course at Albany.

"When they first designed it, all of the holes were about 260 yards long. They had been staking things out and you just couldn't get a feel for the distance in the woods," Hershberg recalled, with a laugh. "I said it would have been great if they wanted a par three course but obviously they didn't."

Hershberg's contributions as a mediator between the two pros also were called into play. "Ed wanted to put pot bunkers all over the course. I think the only one that's still there is on the 12th. And he loved what we called "EBMs"—Ed Bosse Mounds. We had a budget to work within, and I think they both understood that."

While Bosse, Smith and Hershberg were presenting their early designs, the mayor's office was beginning to feel the heat from several pressure groups opposed to the course expansion. Initially, the city had hoped to include an Olympic-sized swimming pool, playground and revamped tennis courts, as well as a new clubhouse, in the project. But the implied message they were getting from many residents in the course's vicinity was that they didn't necessarily want all that in their back yard.

"We had people saying that they liked the course the way it was. They were saying that the whole city would be driving through their neighborhoods to get there," Barrett said. "There were concerns among the neighbors about the traffic."

Despite some vocal opposition, the city received generally positive community input on the new course, including nearly 100 letters and petitions in favor of the redesign from two neighborhood associations.

But by May 1988, the swimming pool, tennis courts and playground were dropped from the project, victims of tighter budget estimates and the criticism of neighbors. Hershberg said Whalen's original vision was for a "common man's country club," and plans still sit in the engineer's office for creating a smaller par three course or an additional nine holes on the land that made up the majority of the "old course."

"He wanted it to be a public country club with all the amenities—swimming pool, nice tennis courts. A place for all city residents," said Hershberg. "That was his vision."

While the city was trimming down its proposal from an original $4.5 million to $2.9 million, a coalition of environmentalists and course neighbors were banding together to create a more formal opposition group to the course expansion. Calling themselves Citizens for Responsible Recreational Development, the group lobbied the Common Council to stop funding for the construction. The group contended that the city's environmental impact statement did not go far enough in explaining the effect the course would have on the Normanskill Creek. City officials disagreed, saying that a 50-foot buffer zone had been created between the course and the creek.

"It was no less than 50 feet and in most place much more. We would have loved to bring the stream more into play, but we did what was in the best interest of the course. We didn't try to poo poo any of the suggestions that came out of the public hearings," Hershberg said.

Chemicals from years of pesticide application on the greens of the old course also concerned the advocates, although the city "capped" the greens on the recommendation of state DEC. "They (state DEC) recommended some very reasonable measures and we complied with them," Hershberg said.

When the protestors weren't successful in swaying city government, they sued the city in state Supreme Court, eventually losing on appeal. Supreme Court Justice Lawrence E. Kahn rejected the group's initial plea in November 1988, and the appeal was knocked down a month later, clearing the way for the actual course construction to begin.

A year later, the new course was again the target of protestors. This time it was advocates for low-income housing who picketed, saying that money would be better spent on the homeless rather than a new golf course. In an October 1989 *Times Union* article, Barrett defended the city's funding for the new course and outlined what the Whalen government was doing for the homeless. "I would hate to see this trend toward improvements in parks and recreation come to a screeching halt because I do believe we have broad public support," he said. "The quality of life in the city is directly related to improvements in the parks and recreation area."

As the decades turned from the 1980s to the 1990s, work began in earnest on the construction. With the plans finalized and the trio of Hershberg, Smith and Bosse overseeing the work, Clark Construction began the earth moving required to shape the holes of the "new course." Although it's tough to picture now, many of the formerly forested acres required a significant amount of reshaping to accommodate the new holes. The land along the banks along the Normanskill—especially at the 15th and 16th—was altered significantly.

Several golfers couldn't resist the temptation to walk out and take a look at the construction while it was taking place. Ed Huba, the unofficial historian of the course, shot several rolls of film of the work and has some great pictures of the 17th as it was being carved out of the woods. Lou Weinman, another Muny golfer from the late 1950s, had just undergone open heart surgery in 1991 and his doctor recommended a healthy regimen of walking. "I came out here to walk around and I had a four iron with me. Well, I got stuck out there at the creek hole in the mud. I thought, great, they'll find me out here in a few days still stuck in this goddamn mud." Lou eventually made it out without assistance.

Golf was still played on the old course through the 1990 and 1991 seasons, but it was obvious something much more interesting was happening in the nearby, newly-seeded fairways.

With a new head pro and superintendent, the New Course at Albany officially opened on July 13, 1991. Ron Armstrong, then the *Times Union* golf correspondent, called it "the prettiest public layout this observer has seen in the Capital District." A beaming Mayor Whalen was the master of ceremonies when the first ball was struck for the inaugural tournament.

"Mayor Whalen was passionate about several things in life. He loved Ireland, rowing on Hudson, but he was equally enthralled by the game of golf," said Barrett. "This course is one of his legacies as mayor. Not only did he renovate the course, but he brought in the people who could truly make it a professional operation. I hope he's remembered as the one who had the vision to make this all happen."

City Champions

The Mayor Thacher Trophy (later the Mayor Corning Trophy) was handed out annually to the winner of the fall city championship tournament. Course pro Jerry Dwyer held a variety of events throughout the golfing season, but the spring handicap tourney and the Mayor's Cup in the fall were considered the most prominent.

Five golfers "retired" the Mayor's Cup by winning it three times—Frank Cummings, Joe Ruszas, Tom Delaney, Frank Hoeffner and Joe Rafferty. The format consisted of a medal play qualifying round. The top 16 qualifiers then entered match play, with the victor taking home the trophy.

The Mayor's Cup city championship died with the passing of Dwyer, and was not re-established until the course was reconstructed in the late 1980s. The tourney became a stroke play affair when it was re-established in 1991. In the 1990s, one golfer achieved what no other city champ had up to that point. Between 1997 and 2001, Jim Toomey won the city championship four times. With his victory in 2002, Doug Kilmer also joined the list of golfers winning the Mayor's Cup on three separate occasions.

"That first year, we played the city championship in October. We had to wait until the end of the year because the golf course really wasn't ready. It was so cold out. Everyone had down jackets on," remembers Vidulich.

These days, the Mayor's Cup tournament is held, weather permitting, in late July.

According to newspaper reports, a women's city championship was also held throughout the 1930s and 1940s. They also may have been contested in later decades but no records or reports exist of winners or

runners up. When the "New Course" was created, one woman dominated the tournament; Beth Fredericks won seven consecutive titles
and eight of the first ten contested.

1932—No Tournament

1933—Frank Cummings

1934—Frank Cummings

1935—Frank Cummings

1936—Dave Duclos

1937—Joe Ruszas

1938—John Cummings/Clare Graves

1939—John Flanagan

1940—Joe Ruszas

1941—Curtis Gammon

1942—Jim Williams

1943—Joe Ruszas

1944—Mike Cipollo

1945—Charley Ruszas

1946—Tom Delaney

1947—Tom Delaney

1948—Peter Van Kampen

1949—Peter Van Kampen

1950—Tom Delaney

1951—Bart Welch

1952—Ken Cameron

1953—Ralph Taggart

1954—Frank Hoeffner

1955—Frank Hoeffner

1956—Jack Reilly

1957—Frank Hoeffner

1958—Joe Rafferty

1959—Joe Rafferty

1960—John Smith

1961—Joe Rafferty

1962—Doug Rutnik

1963—Andy Kroms

1964—Andy Kroms

1965—Tom Venter

1966—Charles Murphy Jr.

1967—No Tournament

1968—No Tournament

1969—No Tournament

1970—No Tournament

1971—No Tournament

1972—No Tournament

1973—No Tournament

1974—No Tournament

1975—No Tournament

1976—No Tournament

1977—No Tournament

1978—No Tournament

1979—No Tournament

1980—No Tournament

1981—No Tournament

1982—No Tournament

1983—No Tournament

1984—No Tournament

1985—No Tournament

1986—No Tournament

1987—No Tournament

1988—No Tournament

1989—No Tournament

1990—No Tournament

1991—Jim Franco	Beth Fredericks
1992—Adam Hershberg	Beth Fredericks
1993—Bill Simpson	Beth Fredericks
1994—Bill Simpson	Beth Fredericks
1995—Doug Kilmer	Beth Fredericks
1996—Doug Kilmer	Beth Fredericks
1997—Jim Toomey	Beth Fredericks
1998—Jim Toomey	Patty Baynes
1999—Jim Toomey	Beth Fredericks
2000—Joe Gadani	Peg Jones
2001—Jim Toomey	Beth Fredericks
2002—Doug Kilmer	Jamie Hall

0-595-26450-6